THE SOUL OF PSYCHOSYNTHESIS

The Seven Core Concepts

By Kenneth Sørensen

"Psychosynthesis is like a tree that keeps growing and producing new leaves and fruits with each passing year. The health of any tree depends on the quality and depth of its roots and Kenneth Sorensen provides us with an excellent source of nourishment to stimulate and revitalize the roots of Psychosynthesis formed by Assagioli's seven core concepts. I appreciate the clear and compelling presentation of the soul of Psychosynthesis and this book reassures and confirms that the spirit of the new psychology is truly alive and well."

Michael Lindfield (Co-founder, Science of Group Work Initiative and President, Meditation Mount, Ojai California)

"We all agree that our world is entering a new epoch: together with the disruption of previuos life forms, not suitable any more to grant human beings a joyful and creative life, we can recognize glimpses of new and more suitable models. Kenneth introduces in this book the seven Pillars of Psychosynthesis, which allow it to be an outpost among the instruments for a radical reconstruction of life on the Planet.

The way he does it, deep and clear at the same time, is a contribution not only to a psychological vision, but to the reconstruction of life on our Planet. Thank you Kenneth!"

Marina Bernardi (President of the Community of Living Ethics, Italy, and co-founder of Science of Group Work initiative)

"Kenneth Sørensen is a Psychosynthesis Psychotherapist, Spiritual Teacher and Author and the ideal person to write precisely this book, The Soul of Psychosynthesis. Here he brings us the essence of a spiritual, therapeutic and practical approach to life. He has written a rare and extremely competent book that offers a wealth and depth of detail, as well as crystal clear insights about Assagioli's Transpersonal Psychology and synthetic therapy. Simply put, it's about the essential qualities of freedom, presence, power, focus, flow, abundance and love. Yet at the same time we are introduced to a diverse craft, an art of living and transformative path of development for the individual. I highly recommend this jewel of a book to anyone who feels attracted to deep personal growth, psychotherapy and spirituality, and who wants to know about Psychosynthesis!"

Søren Hauge, spiritual teacher and author

"Assagioli's psychosynthesis spreads far and wide. It is ambitious in scope and subject matter. For this reason it may be hard at times to understand its essence – with the risk of being lost in the details. Kenneth Sørensen does a great job of summarizing in a short and well-researched book the essential aspects of psychosynthesis, offering an overview that will allow the reader to grasp its main themes in theory and practice, as well as its historical development."

Piero Ferrucci, is an international bestselling author, a psychotherapist and philosopher

Copyright: Kentaur Forlag 2016
Author: Kenneth Sørensen
Translator: Anja Fløde Bjørlo
Printed at: IngramSpark
Layout: Lottethori.no
Cover Photo: Anna Lund Sørensen
Kentaur Forlag: www.psykosyntese.dk
1. Edition
EAN 9788792252173
ISBN: 978-87-92252-17-3

This book is dedicated to Roberto Assagioli

TABLE OF CONTENT

INTRODUCTION

Since completing my MA in Psychosynthesis (Sørensen, 2008), I have wanted to write a book about Roberto Assagioli's system of psychological and spiritual development. A number of questions which I could not examine at the time remained unanswered. Shortly before his death Assagioli (1888-1974) defined seven core concepts which he saw as the essence of Psychosynthesis. Yet in my reading I could find nothing elaborating these concepts. There was, it seemed, a gap in the literature of Psychosynthesis exploring the core of Assagioli's teaching[1].

I wanted to write a book about the *soul* of Psychosynthesis focusing on Assagioli's vision and research that would also offer my own insights based on years of experience working with personal and spiritual development. It seemed clear that Assagioli's seven core concepts could be linked to seven developmental ways: Freedom, Presence, Power, Focus, Flow, Abundance, and Love. These core concepts and developmental ways form the main focus of this book.

The task would be challenging. Assagioli's psychology is widely inclusive and contains numerous philosophical and psychological perspectives; one can easily get lost in cosmic thoughts concerning creation and our place in it. I also recognized an issue with Assagioli's metaphysics. Psychosynthesis meets all the criteria characterising the Integral Model of the American thinker Ken Wilber, which he defines in relation to his ideas on Integral Spirituality. Psychosynthesis, then, could also be located within the framework of a particular philosophical tradition, something I could not address in my MA.

When reading the Psychosynthesis literature written after Assagioli's death, we often find it compared to a wide variety of metaphysical and philosophical schools, for example yoga, Jewish mysticism, Gnosticism, Neo-Platonism, Theosophy and other esoteric traditions. This makes sense. Assagioli was an integral thinker who embraced and explored many different philosophies. Yet it also makes the task of defining the essence of his Psychosynthesis difficult. If the aim of this book is too be clear, the question of the metaphysics of Psychosynthesis must be addressed.

---

1   John Firman, who died in 2008, has been one of the most creative Psychosynthesis thinkers since Assagioli. He has discussed the seven core concepts in depth, but is very critical of many of Assagioli's ideas. He is suggesting some fundamental changes to Assagioli's theories of the Personality and Development. See Firman 1991, 2004, and Sørensen, 2008.

In the introduction to his book *Psychosynthesis – A Collection of Basic Writings* Roberto Assagioli writes:

"Psychosynthesis does not aim nor attempt to give a metaphysical or theological explanation of the great Mystery – it leads to the door, but stops here."
(1975, p. 6-7)

In the same place he writes that Psychosynthesis is "neutral to the various religious forms," because it is based on science. This is certainly debatable. Reading Assagioli's books and articles, it becomes clear that his work is steeped in metaphysical considerations. He opens the door wide to ideas of Cosmic Synthesis, Emanation, Involution and Evolution, Atman, Brahman, Universal Self, etc.

Assagioli's approach to spirituality is clearly theistic. God, Brahman, the Universal Self, is a reality for him. These concepts are not neutral and it would be difficult to integrate, say, a classic Buddhist view within this philosophical framework. Assagioli was a human being who explored the great mystery himself, and he makes it clear that his psychology is based on his own phenomenological experience.

I believe the best description of Assagioli's metaphysics is *Evolutionary Panentheism*. This is a concept that Wilber and the co-founder of Esalen Institute, Michael Murphy, use to define their philosophy. In his article on Evolutionary Panentheism Murphy shows how some of history's greatest intellectual giants have arrived at this concept. They have used different names, but enough common features recur to link them (Murphy, 2012).

Evolutionary means that God (Brahman, the Spirit, the One) permeates *and* transcends the universe. God's presence in creation is both transcendent *and* immanent. God is in everything, but is greater than the created universe. It is through evolution- and therefore humanity – that God's inherent potential unfolds. According to this theory the human soul, and all other beings, "emanate" from God or "Pleroma" (psychologically the human Self.) The word emanation comes from the Latin "emanare" which means "flowing from," in this case, God's abundance. All creatures have emanated from the same divine Source and have journeyed down through the various levels of consciousness into the physical world. Here man "forgets" his origins. The unconscious / conscious yearning for this original unity creates the desire in man to return to the Source, and this urge drives evolution. The purpose of our being is to awaken to the divine potential we are here to unfold and manifest.

In connection with the publication of this book I have compiled a series of quotations from Assagioli's books and articles for readers who want to verify the background of my thoughts. These clearly show that Assagioli based his Psychosynthesis on Evolutionary Panentheism. (Sørensen, 2016) In this book I will include quotations from Assagioli demonstrating his belief that God's transcendent being also is an immanent presence in creation, and that the universe is created and maintained through involution and evolution. The Transpersonal Self or the Soul has an integral role in this cosmic dance.

Does it follow then that one must "believe" in Panentheism to practice Psychosynthesis? Not according to Assagioli and the spirit of Psychosynthesis. As he writes:

"Psychosynthesis is a scientific conception, and as such it is neutral towards the various religious forms and the various philosophical doctrines, excepting only those which are materialistic and therefore deny the existence of spiritual realities." (1975, p. 6-7)

Even though Assagioli let his own metaphysical conceptions shine through, does not mean that students of Psychosynthesis cannot entertain their own thoughts about it. Personally, I am primarily interested in the practical application of Psychosynthesis, how it can help create greater harmony, fellowship and goodwill in the world. I've yet to find a better way to communicate a practical spiritual psychology than Psychosynthesis. I've trained managers, engineers, and Psychosynthesis practitioners, and the explanatory power of Assagioli's simple 'Egg Diagram' is unique. Its usefulness in psychotherapy is, I believe, unrivalled, and is especially effective when working with crisis.

Simplicity is the key to great ideas. Out of great complexity a simple essence can be distilled, and may contain great explanatory power. It is my hope this simplicity will emerge in the course of the following chapters.

I wanted to write a book loyal to Assagioli's original ideas, yet useful to Psychosynthesis Psychotherapy training. When I became Director of Training and Education at the Norwegian Institute of Psychosynthesis, we decided to develop the training around Assagioli's seven core concepts, so the need for this book became urgent.

I embark on the task with great humility. I don't claim to provide "the truth about

Psychosynthesis." Assagioli said he had only created the beginning and that he did not want to establish dogmas. Psychosynthesis evolves and will continue to evolve. Yet it is founded on certain basic assumptions and these are my starting point. This book is my attempt, in good faith, to get to the core of the unique psychology Assagioli developed over a century ago. I am indebted to the many Psychosynthesis practitioners who have gone before me, to Piero Ferrucci, Diana Whitmore and John Firman, to mention a few names central to the development of Psychosynthesis. To what these and others have given I offer my own insights based on my extensive spiritual practice and experience as Psychosynthesis Psychotherapist.

Assagioli was an enthusiastic supporter of Psychoanalysis, but already in 1910 he criticized some of Freud's theories in his doctoral thesis on Psychoanalysis.

He presented his ideas in various journals, and in 1934 he published an overview of Psychosynthesis. Assagioli was decades ahead of Humanistic and Transpersonal Psychology, which first appeared in the 50s and 60s. Assagioli, then, was a contributor to three revolutions in psychology: the Psychoanalytic, the Humanistic and the Transpersonal.

He passes on a formidable heritage to those inspired by his work. I hope that my contribution can shed new light on his legacy and point the way towards new evolutionary possibilities.

Finally I want to thank my translator, Anja Fløde Bjørlo for this wonderful translation.

Kenneth Sørensen, Copenhagen, 2016

CHAPTER I

THE SOUL OF PSYCHOSYNTHESIS
– The seven core concepts

"Even if Psychosynthesis is presented as a synthesis of different therapeutic and educational approaches it is important to remember that is has its own original and central essence." (Assagioli)

I have chosen the title *The Soul of Psychosynthesis* for this book because Psychosynthesis is known as "a Psychology with a Soul". The etymological meaning of 'Psychology' is "the study of the Soul", but where mainstream psychology largely denies the existence of a soul as a spiritual core, Psychosynthesis places the soul at its centre. I have also chosen the title because my aim is to identify what is the core, the essence or the soul in Psychosynthesis.

Psychosynthesis presents so broad and inclusive a view of humanity and our spiritual journey that we can easily lose sight of its central ideas. In *Psychosynthesis – A Collection of Basic Writings*, his first book, Assagioli uses a wide range of ideas and psychotherapeutic techniques from many different sources. This can easily confuse a reader and give the impression that more or less everything can be included under the Psychosynthesis umbrella.

Interviewing Assagioli shortly before his death in 1974, Sam Keen, an editor from Psychology Today, asked: "What are the limits with Psychosynthesis?" And Assagioli answered: "The limit of Psychosynthesis is that it has no limits. It is too extensive, too comprehensive. Its weakness is that it accepts too much. It sees too many sides at the same time and that is a drawback". (Keen, 1974)

This is a positive admission, and is true exactly because Psychosynthesis *is* so integrative. It is an attempt to fuse the deep wisdom of the Self coming from the East with modern western psychology and its insight into the unconscious.

THE CENTRAL IDEAS OF PSYCHOSYNTHESIS

Nevertheless certain core ideas underpin all of Assagioli's writings and connect all the disparate parts. These are: synthesis; the evolution of consciousness; energy psychology; and the manifestation of spirit. These themes can also be found in Evolutionary Panentheism, the metaphysical philosophy on which Assagioli seems to have based his work. (Sørensen, 2015)

To understand these themes we must look at the big picture. In this way the many techniques and theoretical elements can be seen as parts of an overarching process.

In Psychosynthesis Assagioli describes this perspective:

"From a still wider and more comprehensive point of view, universal life itself appears to us as a struggle between multiplicity and unity – a labor and an aspiration towards union. We seem to sense that – whether we conceive it as a divine Being or as a cosmic energy – the Spirit working upon and within all creation is shaping it into order, harmony, and beauty, uniting all beings (some willing but the majority as yet blind and rebellious) with each other through links of love, achieving – slowly and silently, but powerfully and irresistibly – the Supreme Synthesis". (1975, p. 31)

Synthesis is hence a law of nature. It is the aim of life, a developmental process which governs all living beings. Its intention is to unite all living beings with their divine source through the energy of Love and Will (1974, ch. 8-10) Assagioli relates this law to the scientific principle of 'syntropy', referring to the mathematician Luigi Fantappiè as well as to Buckminster Fuller and Teilhard de Chardin. (1974, p. 32)

The Evolution of Consciousness. Assagioli presupposes the existence of a creative divine intelligence driving the unfolding of life, expressing itself in us as a longing for a greater and all-embracing love. This inner power directs our evolution through certain universal stages of development, from body, psyche, and soul to spiritual consciousness. It is the evolution of consciousness from Ego-centric to Cosmic-centric love. These stages are described in Chapter III. Not only humans evolve, all of creation does too. For Assagioli our development moves through "various levels of reality" or "energy fields", from the physical to the psychological, and then to the spiritual and transcendental. According to Assagioli these energy fields are an "essential aspects of Psychosynthesis." (Undated 2)

Assagioli is saying: "that the great evolutionary process culminated in the mineral kingdom, as far as we know, and then started the reverse movement or process of evolution. Slightly optimistic we can say that we are half way. We have passed through mineral, plant, animal and partially the human kingdom. So we have to continue this evolutionary work towards the "One", but it is still far away. (Undated 2)

Assagioli refers to the evolution of consciousness several places, (1975, p. 214, 1974, p. 166)[2] and he describes this evolution in individual as a well as in social terms. "The psychological life of a nation corresponds to a great extent to that which is *unconscious* in individuals. Modern investigation of unconscious psychological activities has ascertained that these are chiefly instinctive, emotional and imaginative. ... The conscious part of an individual corresponds, in a people, to a minority constituted by its thinkers (philosophers, historians, psychologists, sociologists and other scientists), who endeavour to develop the self-consciousness of the nation, to interpret its past, to assess its present conditions and to point to the future. ... It happens also at times that these great individuals become inspired not only from their own Selves, but also from the soul of their nation, which uses them as its instruments and representatives, in order to reveal itself and achieve its group purpose." (Assagioli, 1965, Undated 4) As mentioned, in this respect Assagioli's psychology is closely related to that of Ken Wilber and the contemporary research Wilber draws on.[3]

Psychosynthesis, then, is a psychology which deliberately seeks to cooperate with evolution. Humanity is the first species on this planet to have become conscious of the evolutionary process. Psychosynthesis achieves this cooperation through its psychological approach to Harmony and Unity. Synthesis is a gradual process. It begins in our inner world, first unconsciously then consciously when we embark on our own personal and transpersonal psychosynthesis. Its goal is the harmonization and reconciliation of the conflicts and divisions we experience in ourselves, with others and the planet as a whole.

Energy Psychology. Psychosynthesis is an Energy Psychology. Assagioli saw the need for "a science of the Self, of its energies, its manifestations, of how these energies can be released, how they can be contacted, how they can be utilized for constructive and therapeutic work." (1975, p. 194) Assagioli admits that 'hard' empirical evidence for such a 'science' may still be lacking, yet contemporary research on consciousness and its effects on the brain related to the scientific study of 'Mindfulness' -which Assagioli was unaware of – gives clear indications of a Mind-Body connection.

Through Psychosynthesis we gain extensive phenomenological access to the world of energies. We can experience these worlds directly through introspection

---

2   There are many references to evolution in the collection of quotes *'Psychosynthesis and Evolutionary Panentheism'*.

3   Read my MA-dissertation: *Integral Psychosynthesis*, a comparison of Ken Wilber and Roberto Assagioli: http://psykosyntese.dk/a-198/

and through Psychosynthesis techniques learn how to direct our physical, psychological and spiritual forces. The work with and within energies is a prerequisite of the work of Psychosynthesis.

The Manifestation of Spirit. Finally I want to highlight that Psychosynthesis is not necessarily about having a "mystical experience". Its aim is not to withdraw from the world, to 'transcend' it and reach some other "divine world". For Assagioli Psychosynthesis is about being *in this* world fully. It is about making use of all the creative resources we have at our disposal. In this way we can contribute to evolution of life. (1975, p. 207) For Assagioli, Synthesis is a union which includes the body because it is through it that spiritual energies can manifest in the world. The grand vision is of the manifestation of spirit on earth; it is a vision Assagioli shares with many contemporary evolutionists, especially the Integral Yoga of the Eastern mystic Sri Aurobindo.

ASSAGIOLI'S "LAST WILL "

From this general overview of Psychosynthesis, let's move to a more detailed account of its unique qualities, in particularly those relevant for Psychosynthesis training and education. We begin with an important document Assagioli wrote shortly before his death.

In his announcement to Psychosynthesis institutes around the world (see Appendix) Assagioli said that Psychosynthesis has "its own original and central essence". According to John Firman and Ann Gila (2007), a few months before his death Assagioli left behind a document outlining the essentials for Psychosynthesis training, understood by some as his "last will".

Assagioli maintained that Psychosynthesis is an experiential approach to the "facts" on which Psychosynthesis rest. Anyone can experiment with these facts in the laboratory of consciousness and it is essential for the understanding of Psychosynthesis to undertake such experiments. As Assagioli writes:

"While Psychosynthesis is offered as a synthesis of various therapies and educational approaches, it is well to keep in mind that it possesses its own original and central essence. This is so as not to present a watered-down and distorted version, or one over-coloured by the concepts and tendencies of the various contemporary schools. Certain fundamental facts exist, and their relative conceptual elaboration, deep experience and understanding are central, and constitute the sine qua non of Psychosynthesis training.

These experiences are:

1. Disidentification

2. The personal self

3. The Will: good, strong, skilful

4. The Ideal Model

5. Synthesis (in its various aspects)

6. The Superconscious

7. The Transpersonal Self (in the majority of cases it is not possible to have a complete experience of this, but it's good to have a theoretical knowledge of the characteristics and experience of its guidance)."[4]

These are the seven "facts" and fundamental features of Psychosynthesis that must be part of Psychosynthesis training and its education syllabus. These core concepts are what we can call "the soul of Psychosynthesis."

As understood by Assagioli, any authentic practice and training in Psychosynthesis must involve a direct experience of these areas. This doesn't mean that Psychosynthesis can't or won't develop. Naturally it must and will otherwise it would not be psychosynthetic. Yet the seven core concepts form the cornerstone of Psychosynthesis and represent the foundation and starting point for the training.

In the same document Assagioli defines five relevant areas for the application of Psychosynthesis:

"The therapeutic (psychotherapy; doctor-patient relations); personal integration and actualization (realization of one's own potentialities); the educational (psychosynthesis by parents and by educators in school of all degrees); the interpersonal (marriage, couples etc.); the social (right social relations within groups and between groups)".

The above must be based on personal psychosynthesis, the first-person experience of integrating the seven core concepts in one's life. Psychosynthesis is oriented toward experience; it is a practical approach to personal and spiritual develop-

---

4   See appendix

ment, and can only be understood and communicated through own experiences. What comes out of the practice of these core concepts is interesting. What, for example, are the direct benefits of practicing disidentification and developing the self and the Will, etc.?

I believe that each core concept reveals a developmental path- or way- to seven different dimensions of consciousness, to freedom, presence, power, focus, flow, abundance and love. The aim of this book is to show how this is so.

THE SEVEN CORE CONCEPTS IN PSYCHOSYNTHESIS

I will now briefly outline how I understand Assagioli's seven core concepts, based on quotes from Assagioli and my personal experiences and reflection. The following chapters will provide examples of how we can work with these concepts as part of the process of personal and transpersonal psychosynthesis, as well as in a therapeutic setting.

Disidentification – The Way to Freedom

The mother of all the other Psychosynthesis techniques is disidentification; this is acquired through the Self-Identification exercise. Assagioli advised using the Self-Identification exercise "as early as possible" because it gives the practitioner the skills needed to use the other psychotherapeutic techniques. (1975, p. 119)

The aim of the disidentification exercise is to discover the self. Assagioli defines our identity, the self or the conscious "I", as "a point of pure self-consciousness". (1975, p. 18) Our sense of identity is often conditioned by our social roles (parental, professional, gender) or by different thoughts, feelings and sensations. Consequently we do not recognise who we really are. Assagioli points out that our true identity is not found in any of these roles; it is the observer which is *aware of the content of consciousness,* and which is experiencing and expressing itself through these roles.

Our roles and the content of consciousness constantly change, while consciousness itself and the 'observer' is a permanent, unchanging centre.

To experience this permanent, unchanging centre of consciousness we have to disidentify from our roles and the passing content of consciousness. We have to "take a step back" with our mind and experience thoughts, feelings and sensation as objects that can be observed. This is difficult. Our unconscious and semi-conscious identifications are hard to abandon, and even this is still only the first step.

Fundamentally we want to identify with consciousness *itself*, the subject and the observer, and no longer lose ourselves in its various contents.

Why is this important? Because, Assagioli, says, "We are dominated by everything with which our self becomes identified. We can dominate and control everything from which we disidentify ourselves". (1975, p. 111) In other words it is a question of becoming *free* enough to master everything that we contain.

Assagioli was inspired by the Eastern practice of *Vipassana* (Keen, 1974). In Vipassana and Advaita Vedanta we disidentify from the objects of consciousness in order to reach a direct experience of the self as pure consciousness. Psychosynthesis, then, can be seen as a radical psycho-spiritual practice, similar to some yogic practices, and it offers techniques to achieve this level of consciousness (1975, p. 19).

To awaken to and recognise ourselves as pure self-awareness is a process and a journey. Although the self/subject is always potentially present, it is usually hidden behind layers of identification, with thoughts, feelings and bodily sensations. These layers must first be recognized and detached from before our identity as pure self-awareness can emerge.

In order to reach this level Assagioli developed the Self-Identification exercise (1975, p. 111). Disidentifying with the body, emotions and thoughts enables us to identify with consciousness itself. Through observing the body, feelings, and thoughts we recognise that we are not these but are the 'observer'. This leads to greater freedom. Instead of mechanically following certain roles we can now choose whatever we wish to identify with. It is a way of awakening to the pure consciousness of the self. It is a technique to achieve freedom because the self is open and without content. We will go into the self-identification process in more detail further on.

Disidentification is a prerequisite for identification with the self as pure self-awareness. This takes us to Assagioli's second core concept: the self.

The self – The Way to Presence

Assagioli describes the self in different ways. He speaks of the personal self, the conscious "I" and even the ego. (1975, p. 7, 18) Assagioli's use of the word ego is something very different from other psychological disciplines, and this can create confusion. Here I will refer to the personal self as the self or the observer, and we should remember that self, as defined by Assagioli, always means "a centre of pure self-awareness and will". (1974, p. 216) This self is not a thought, a feeling or sensation, but a dynamic consciousness which can observe and learn how to master its content.

The will occupies the next section. Here let's focus on the self as pure self-awareness and see why, compared to other Western psychologies, the psychosynthetic approach is unique. Experiencing the self as pure self-awareness usually does not happen spontaneously. It requires introspection and the ability to disidentify from the 'stream of consciousness'. Most of the time we identify with everything that passes through the mind, and so we completely ignore consciousness itself. This is a point to which Assagioli often refers (1975, p. 112). Why, then, is pure self-awareness so important?

The goal of disidentification is to find a centre, around which we can integrate the resources available to the personality. Psychosynthesis is precisely the process by which we recognize, develop and unfold all our psychological resources. The self is such a centre. It is through the presence of the self we awake as the observer – presence as focused self-awareness. Through this faculty we can achieve a harmonious and liberated life.

Identifying with the observer gives us a vantage point from which we can recognize all that our consciousness contains. We have found the source of light which illuminates and clarifies. To be truly free we must be able to make choices based on conscious awareness of our resources, needs and values. Otherwise, we are driven by unconscious desires, fears and emotions which may indeed not come from our selves. When we discover the self as the observer, we have the opportunity to evaluate our actions. This should not inhibit spontaneous self-expression, but ensures that we act out of our deepest values and authentic needs.

Self-awareness is 'presence': the ability to be awake and aware here and now in a non-attached manner. It is a loving presence that contains, observes and interacts with the contents of consciousness. The development of the self is therefore a development towards greater presence: the ability to be completely grounded in one's self and one's awakened being. We will expand on this later and give examples from 'Awareness Based Therapy'.

The Will – The Way to Power

Assagioli's third core concept is the will. Of all the great psychological pioneers, none have written so extensively on the will as Assagioli. That Assagioli connects the will directly to the self, makes it clear that it is one of the key features of Psychosynthesis.

As mentioned, Assagioli describes the self as "a centre of pure self-awareness and will". The experience of the will is according to Assagioli an inner existential fact, and involves a three stage process. You first recognize the existence of the will. Then you discover that you *have a will*. The third stage is complete when you realize yourself *as being a will* (1974, p. 7). It is during this last stage that we according to Assagioli discover that: "I AM A WILL; I AM A CONSCIOUS, POTENT, DYNAMIC WILL "(1974 p. 176), which is the central aim of Self-realization. Before this process begins we can feel that we have no will and that life develops as a result of chance events and unconscious impulses.

When the will is so closely linked to our identity it is obvious why it is first and foremost connected with the will-to-be-self. The will-to-be-self is our urge and our longing for authenticity and the need to be a unique individual. When we connect the will *directly to our identity*, as the will-to-be-self, the reality of the will becomes existential much sooner, that is, it is felt as a direct inner experience. I will expand on this point in the chapter on the will.

When our will is the will of the self, it becomes a dynamic power through which we express ourselves. When Assagioli speaks of the will, he means something quite different than the "Victorian will" and the repression of our desires and sexual drives. Assagioli believes that if sufficiently developed, the will can become a central force directing and regulating desire according to the self's authentic self-image.

The will is not desire. More times than not our desires run counter to our will. For example, when we don't want to do something, because we know it will be humiliating, but we do it anyway because of the power of the desire. The will is associated with conscious choice and consent, the observer's consent. The will is basically the will-to-be-self. But we are not always able to express this will, because we have come to rely on – or are even addicted to- a behaviour that is not consistent with our authentic self-image.

If we want to be ourselves, we must develop our connection to our will. Self-awareness (the observer) is an indispensable prerequisite for individuality, because it creates awareness. The will is equally important because it provides us with the strength and freedom to be ourselves. The will opens up a developmental path towards an exponentially greater power, because there is no greater power than being a unique self.

The will is often the last psychological function we discover. It can be frightening to become who we are because we have to learn how to stand alone. Freedom comes with a price. We must deliberately reject the herd instinct and its dependency on social roles, conformity and "normality". The will gives us the courage to step away from herd mentality into self-awareness and individual expression. It is not enough to recognize our uniqueness; we must *express* it in our choices. True identity is not something we just *have*; it is something we must manifest via our choices and expressions. We need the will as the power to assemble, integrate and express the many resources at our disposal. It is through the will-to-be-a-self that we create a consistent direction in our lives and start acting as an independent and free human being. Assagioli refers to this achievement as personal psychosynthesis.

The Ideal Model – the Way to Focus

The fourth core concept Assagioli mentions in his statement is the Ideal Model. As with the self-identification exercise the Ideal Model is an important tool in our work of creating a harmonious and integrated personality. It is a visualization technique in which you create an image of what you can be. You then focus your resources to realise, or manifest, this image. The overall objective is synthesis, the gathering and coordination of all our inner powers towards a single unity. It aims at developing a liberated, vibrant and spontaneous ability to actualise all our creative resources. The Ideal Model exercise must be applied in the larger context of the Seven Core Concepts. In his statement Assagioli's writes:

"Psychosynthesis is not identified with any technique or practice. Despite the fact that in group work use is often made of guided imagination and visualization exercises, Psychosynthesis can by no means be levelled down to these techniques."

The Ideal Model presents a realistic image of what you may be, when you focus your will and enthusiasm to becoming it. An Ideal Model is an authentic self-image guiding one's imagination and patterns of behaviour. It is a technique that combines self-awareness, will, imagination and passion with the aim to become the best version of you.

This technique makes use of nature's own design, in the sense that we already contain a number of self-images and self-perceptions which we have consciously and unconsciously "recorded" during the course of our lives. These inner self images control our lives because they make us act according to their content. Assagioli refers to psychological research which supports this notion and the following psychological law: "Images, mental pictures and ideas tend to produce the physical conditions and external acts that correspond to them." (1974, p. 51) He is referring to several psychological laws, but with regards to the Ideal Model this is the most important.

Marketing and advertising are well aware of this law and frequently use it to manipulate consumers.

Assagioli mentions six categories of false self-images (1975, p. 167), including self-concepts that either underestimate or overestimate ourselves. These are often rooted in our need to adjust to our environment. Psychosynthesis aims to expose these false self-images and to redefine and create a new Ideal Model, "the image of himself that he can and will eventually reach when Psychosynthesis is completed." (Assagioli, 1975, p. 164)

The Ideal Model uses the imagination, one of the seven psychological functions Assagioli includes in his Psychosynthesis. Creative visualization is a powerful technique. It can synthesize all the other psychological functions. (1975, p. 144) When we visualize an image of what we realistically may be, we develop concentration and will. We awaken feelings and desires that motivate us to actualize the image. This strengthens the image which in turn increases our desire. We create a new personality around the Ideal Model, based on our knowledge of available psychological resources and what is meaningful to us. This work strengthens our focus on becoming an authentic self, and working with the Ideal Models is in itself a path to greater focus. Being an authentic self is the most important goal we can have, because it implies that we express this creative self in joy and for the benefit to ourselves and others.

Assagioli recommends that we should start with the Ideal Model in order to develop certain psychological qualities. The Ideal Model is useful when we work with the inferior aspects of our nature, helping to achieve more peace, will, empathy or whatever the individual needs. In the chapter on the Ideal Model we will examine how we can apply this powerful technique to create greater focus.

Synthesis – The Way to Flow

Clearly, synthesis has a central focus in Psychosynthesis. As described earlier, it is a law of nature and is expressed as the movement toward harmony, wholeness and unity. We can see this everywhere. It is the energy behind the evolution of consciousness.

Historically, humanity has organized itself into exponentially larger groups. One effect of this is what we today call globalization. This has both good and bad consequences. This movement towards wholeness begins in the individual when the need to "know oneself" emerges. Because of this the resources available to the personality gather around certain goals and values. It seems clear that this need for personal development and Self-realization has never been greater.

When opposing forces collide, whether in oneself or between people, groups or different nations, life turns into conflict, war and struggle. Duality seems inescapable; it appears at all levels of existence: physically, psychologically and spiritually. It is precisely this tension which creates the possibility of harmony through conflict.

We are all familiar with the psychological dualities at play in ourselves and our lives, pleasure-pain, confidence-fear, attraction-repulsion, and so on. Psychosynthesis offers the possibility of harmonizing and managing these conflicts. The guiding rule is that a conflict cannot be solved at the level of consciousness at which it began, but only at a higher level. It is precisely here that the recognition of the observer and our ability to disidentify becomes crucial. When we disidentify from our conflicting poles, a higher level of consciousness (the observer) emerges, through which the recognition, acceptance and creative techniques can be used to reconcile the opposing forces.

For example, when we take on a new challenge, we may find that we react with both excitement and fear. The solution is not to repress the fear, but to address the part of us that is afraid with insight and love. Our fear, when it is transformed, can then cooperate with our excitement and these opposite poles can be synthesized. This does not mean a bland balance between opposing forces but something entirely new, a synthesis, and subsequently a sensible engagement is possible.

The result of synthesis is flow: the spontaneous ability to freely express oneself in the particular area. Working with synthesis is a developmental path that increases 'flow' in many areas of our lives. In the chapter on synthesis we will examine the conditions of 'flow' and how they are created.

The Superconscious

Psychosynthesis is a transpersonal psychology. It speaks of so-called 'peak experiences' which involve the mystical and transcendental levels of consciousness. Throughout history people have had inspirational experiences that in some instances have changed the world. These experiences may be felt as a union with an all-embracing love or as deep insights into existential laws. Although rare these extraordinary experiences are nevertheless as 'natural' as more common experiences, such as hunger, aggression and sexuality.

The Superconscious is Assagioli's sixth core concept in Psychosynthesis. It relates to his focus on the exploration and development of transpersonal states. The Superconscious is an upper floor in our inner house (personality), which contains energies, values and modes that involve holistic and universal experiences. Here we come to understand and directly experience the world as a unified network of energies with which we all are connected.

In the next chapter we will go deeper into Assagioli's Egg Diagram, where he describes the various unconscious levels of the personality. The Superconscious is the higher aspect of the personality. (1975, p. 89) Here we can say that the different levels of consciousness outside ordinary awareness consist of various types of interconnected energy. (1975, p. 200) The Superconscious consists of energies with a higher frequency than that of our "normal" consciousness. (1975, p. 198)

The Superconscious expresses itself through our enlightened poets, politicians, artists, educators, scientists, mystics and creators. These individuals share a universal ethic, and display a genius and depth of insight which have often shaped our civilization and culture. They may be unaware of it, but these individuals are an expression of the spirit of synthesis. They show us the higher spiritual possibilities we all can acquire.

Psychosynthesis has developed methods of tapping into the Superconscious levels in order for their beauty, love and power to become manifest through our creative work. Just as the forces from the Lower Unconscious must be integrated, so too must we integrate our spiritual energies in order for us to actualize all of our human potential. The Superconscious is the soul's inner treasure chamber, where we can find and express an abundance of creative potential. We can say that the techniques connecting us to the Superconscious represent a developmental path towards greater abundance. Instead of filling empty lives, we *create* an abundant life which we share with the world. Assagioli describes this goal as our transpersonal psychosynthesis. More will be said about this in the chapter on the Superconscious.

The Transpersonal Self – the Way to Love

Our focus has been to explore the essential elements of Psychosynthesis so as to get an idea of what is indispensable in Psychosynthesis training and education. Arriving at the Transpersonal Self, Assagioli admits the difficulty in reaching a full experience of the Self. Yet a theoretical understanding of the Transpersonal Self and of its guidance is still important. Assagioli sometimes called the Transpersonal Self the Higher Self, or simply the Self (with a capital S) or the soul. Here I call it the Transpersonal Self or soul.

Many people have experienced the soul and Assagioli writes: "In any case, thousands of individuals, millions perhaps, have had the experience of the Self and have given testimony to it. In India, it is traditionally called the "Atman". Some of the deeper Christian mystics have been aware of it and have called it variously, the "divine spark" of the person, the "apex", the "base", the "centre" and the "innermost essence". (Miller, 1973)

We do not *have* a Transpersonal Self, we *are* this Self. When Assagioli distinguishes between the Personal self and the Transpersonal Self, he does not assume two 'selves'. The Personal self is a pale reflection or emanation of its source, the Transpersonal Self. It is a phenomenological difference, one of experience, between the self of the world of the personality – experienced through the filters of our mind – and the soul in its own transcendental world. The Self is always a centre of pure self-awareness and will, no matter what. Assagioli explains the difference: "The real distinguishing factor between the little self and the higher Self is that the little self is acutely aware of itself as a distinct separate individual, and a sense of solitude or of separation sometimes comes in the existential experience. In contrast, the experience of the spiritual Self is a sense of freedom, of expansion, of communication with other Selves and with reality, and the sense of Universality. It feels itself at the same time individual and universal". (1975, p. 87)

The Transpersonal Self creates the Superconscious (1974, p. 119) with all its creative processes of light, beauty and love. The soul is a static centre of pure being and self-awareness whose energies radiate, in the same way as the sun's do, a comparison Assagioli often makes. We see the sun's rays but not its stable core. (Undated 2)

For Assagioli the soul is a divine living being, and we experience its essence as a quiet intimate connection with all living beings and the cosmos. In the centre of the soul, we discover ourselves as a calm, observing and dynamic presence, a universal and unchanging awareness and consciousness, permanently present in the background. The soul is witness to all our levels of consciousness and processes, which themselves come into being through the soul's emanation and it's will-to-be. The soul is individual. It has a unique purpose: to manifest the universal consciousness through a concrete physical expression. The soul and its emanation represent the relationship between being and becoming. The soul is never anything else but I- amness, but where our personal self is constricted by the body, emotions and thoughts, the "Self is above and beyond the personality and untouched by the mind stream and bodily conditions". (1975, p. 19) "The Self is outside time and above it. It exists and lives in the dimension of the Eternal". (Assagioli, 1973)

The soul is limitless. What we identify with in the world of personality is like a drop of water in an ocean of endless possibilities and resources. The Transpersonal Self can never be fully 'explained'. It transcends factual language, and we can only refer to the quality of the experience. One quality more than anything else describes the soul, and that is love. This love can be called "unity consciousness"; through it the soul experiences a deep connection with all living beings. The soul experiences no separation because it realizes its essential unity with all living beings as an existential fact. Contact with the Transpersonal Self hence opens up a developmental path towards limitless love, a path we will explore further on.

Having given an overview of Assagioli's seven core concepts – and touching on some of his fundamental ideas about Psychosynthesis along the way – in the next two chapters I will present his model of the personality and his developmental theory. This model will be helpful in relating the seven core concepts to the human psycho-spiritual structure and its development.

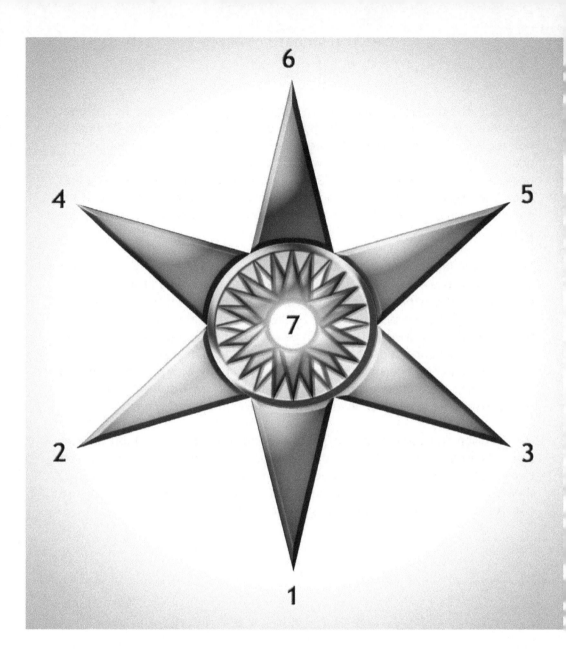

Will   (7)
Intuition   (6)
Thought   (5)
Imagination (4)
Desire   (3)
Feeling   (2)
Sensation   (1)

CHAPTER II

THE PSYCHOSYNTHESIS MODEL OF THE PERSONALITY

"In one of his letters Freud said, "I am interested only in the basement of the human being." Psychosynthesis is interested in the whole building." (Assagioli)

Assagioli presented his Egg Diagram for the first time in 1934 (see below) in an article in the Hibbert Journal with the title *Psicoanalisi e Psicosintesi*. In this article, he presented his theory of the personality based on the Egg Diagram, and the text was later included in his first book: *Psychosynthesis – A Collection of Basic Writings* [5].

Assagioli acknowledges a number of psychoanalytic, existential and spiritual influences that have shaped his thinking about the human personality. We can say his approach is integral, because he seeks to create a "multi-dimensional view of the human personality" in which he is including all theories available at the time. (1975, p. 16)

Assagioli was not the first to use the term "Psychosynthesis". He cites numerous authors who also used it. In his argument

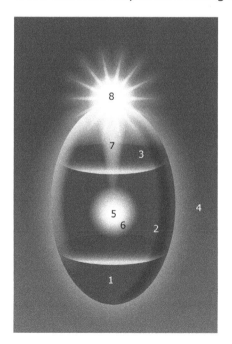

Assagioli's Egg Diagram

1. *Lower Unconscious*
2. *Middle Unconscious*
3. *Higher Unconscious*
4. *Collective unconscious*
5. *The self/Observer*
6. *Field of Consciousness*
7. *The Bridge of Consciousness*
8. *The soul/the Transpersonal Self*

---

5   Roberto Assagioli, *Psychosynthesis – a collection of Basic Writings*. Turnstone Press, 1975.

with what he saw as the "error of one-sidedness" in Freud's theories, C. G. Jung wrote: "If there is a 'Psychoanalysis', then there must also be a 'Psychosynthesis', which creates future events according to the same laws." [6] Nevertheless, Assagioli believed his application of the term was more comprehensive, definitive and technical than other writers.

Assagioli recognizes that the Egg Diagram "is far from perfect and definitive". It provides only a "structural, static, almost 'anatomical' representation of our inner constitution, while it leaves out its dynamic aspect, which is the most important and essential one." (1975, p. 16)

In the next chapter we will look at the developmental theory so here we will address the anatomical aspects of Assagioli's model of the personality. Assagioli's Egg Diagram illustrates and describes the relationship between consciousness and the different levels of energy in the human psyche. As mentioned in Chapter I Assagioli hoped that one day we would have a science of energy. Psychosynthesis is his contribution, and the Egg Diagram is an attempt to describe man as a multidimensional being, containing various levels of awareness and energy. This is according to Assagioli an "essential point of Psychosynthesis." (Undated 2)

When we speak of levels of consciousness, we are referring to physical, emotional, mental and intuitive levels consisting of different types of energies of which we can become conscious. We experience these energies when we sense, feel, think and have intuitive flashes- and what we are conscious of represents only the tip of the iceberg, as Freud discovered. Assagioli divides his diagram into three levels of consciousness, in which we participate more or less, depending on our general level of awareness and where our awareness is directed at any given time.

What resides in the part of the diagram given to the 'unconscious' is not necessarily itself 'unconscious, meaning not available to the conscious mind. We have an on-going connection with a lot of the energies and needs within these areas. This is particularly relevant for level 1 and 2. According to Assagioli: "The basic and normal personal needs concern the lower and middle psychological life; conscious or unconscious." (1974, p. 110) We will return to this point later.

At the centre of the Egg Diagram (5) we find the self, a point of pure self-awareness and will, but often, as previously discussed- we are not usually aware of ourselves as "self-aware observers". We only have a very limited experience of the energies and potentialities we possess. Within the self's field of consciousness (6) we become aware of the various energies within us; we can also call this "the field of

---

6   Jung, in J. Kerr, *A Dangerous Method (2012*, p. 214-5)

attention". We are not aware of everything we know at any given time, naturally, but we bring it to our attention in the field of consciousness (6) when we need it. *You can compare the process to a computer. Most of its processes take place in the hard drive and ROM/RAM storage* (level 1 + 2) and don't appear on the screen (6). What appears on the screen is only what the user chooses to focus on, or what the system (compared here with the unconscious) is programmed to show. Assagioli describes it this way:

"The contents of the Lower Unconscious, new data from parts of the Middle Unconscious and also impulses from the Superconscious pour into this area of awareness."(Miller, 1973)

With this in mind, let's look at the various levels of the unconscious and see what energies, resources and needs they contain. Assagioli has a useful metaphor for the Egg Diagram: he called it a house with many floors, an image Assagioli himself used. When he was asked how Psychosynthesis differed from Psychoanalysis, he said:

"We pay far more attention to the Higher Unconscious and to the development of the Transpersonal Self. In one of his letters Freud said, "I am interested only in the basement of the human being." Psychosynthesis is interested in the whole building. We try to build an elevator which will allow a person access to every level of his personality. After all, a building with only a basement is very limited. We want to open up the terrace where you can sun-bathe or look at the stars. Our concern is the synthesis of all areas of the personality." (Keen, 1974)

THE LOWER UNCONSCIOUS

At the bottom of the diagram (1) we find the Lower Unconscious. I prefer to call this the Basic Unconscious to avoid any negative associations connected to the word "lower". This area corresponds to what psychoanalysts call the unconscious. Physical well-being, discomfort, hunger, sexual needs, desire, aggression, and many pleasant and unpleasant urges all flow up from the lower unconscious and into the field of consciousness affecting the behaviour of the self. Many of these drives are blind and instinctive. They control our habits such as, sleep, eating, and a wide range of physiological processes. Here we store repressed and traumatized experiences from childhood. Certain circumstances re-activate these memories and they emerge as fear, anxiety, shame, pain and various inexplicable inhibitions. These energies are egocentric. They ensure that our basic survival, protection and security needs are met. These are physical drives such as basic instincts, emotions and fantasies related to early childhood. This level of consciousness therefore represents the consciousness of our inner child and other basic patterns – for good or ill.

The Lower Unconscious is incredible vital, and it is essential for us to draw on its vitality as our lives unfold. Through it we create intimate relationships. It is the source of our spontaneity and playfulness. It enables us to face the world confidently, and gives us the energy to fight for what we need. The Lower Unconscious therefore is the foundation upon which the personality rests. In our personal psychosynthesis we explore this level of consciousness and learn how to develop and integrate its valuable resources in our lives.

Insofar as the self is identified with energies of this region, it will be dominated by its requirements, needs and values. Someone whose sole focus is on material security and the safety of the family will draw his or her identity mainly from the Lower Unconscious.

THE MIDDLE UNCONSCIOUS

The contents of the Middle Unconscious (2) are much like those of the waking consciousness of a relatively rational and educated human being, young or adult. [7] Here many of our psychological processes are being organised 'behind the scenes' before being made available to consciousness. As Assagioli writes, they are "those things that are latent, quiescent: or active in our personality but we are not aware of at the moment." (Assagioli, Miller, 1973) This is the region of the Pre-Conscious.

In the Middle Unconscious we find energies associated with our relationships, status and self-esteem. These energies are connected to our higher emotions and rational beliefs about life, such as our political, religious and social attitudes. Here we find the more or less conscious values we have adopted in life as a result of our education and socialisation. Here we store our conscious self-image and establish an identity, which then enable our self-expression and the development of boundaries. We discover here our need for friendship, belonging and for finding our place in a group and society. Through these we develop our creativity and talents supporting our life path. Here too we find inhibitions, fear and frustrations stemming from challenges and trauma of our teens, a time when we develop our self-conscious personality and become adults. These affect our sense of identity

---

7   In the next chapter the Egg Diagram will be connected to Assagioli's theory of Development and Maslow's Hierarchy of Needs, hence the reference to age.

and self-worth, and consequently our relationship to love, work and status.

When the self is identified with this region and has its focus here, the Lower Unconscious is nevertheless active. But unless you have unresolved issues around safety and security, it recedes into background as a focus for identity. If there are such issues, when they are activated, we become fixated here until they are resolved. Our fixations cause "childish" behaviour because they represent unresolved needs from childhood requiring attention. The integration of these energies makes us more reflective and self-aware.

In the upper part of the Middle Unconscious we find more holistic mental energies. These trigger the urge to self-actualize. This is the culmination of the personality, the inspiration to create a truly successful and active life according to the existing values.

THE HIGHER UNCONSCIOUS OR SUPERCONSCIOUS

With the uppermost level of the diagram, the Higher Unconscious or Superconscious (3), we reach the realm of the transpersonal. 'Transpersonal' means 'beyond the personal'. Here experiences and insights expand our consciousness beyond our individual selves and towards the universal, consciousness become *holistic*. We feel ourselves to be an integral part of a whole which is greater than our limited personalities.

An experience of a transpersonal love can dissolve all boundaries and make us feel at one with humanity. Or we experience deep insight into the nature of existence. From this region we receive inspiration for ideas such as Human Rights and feel the need for a universal ethic. Major scientific discoveries, artistic inspirations or the heroic call to sacrifice one's life to a great cause begin at this level of consciousness.

Through the Superconscious we connect with something greater than ourselves, and feel a yearning for deeper meaning and purpose in our lives.

When the self rises to the Superconscious, say in meditation, our sense of identity expands. Yet, influences and inspiration from the Superconscious can also descend and inform our personal conscious, without expanding our identity. We will in chapter nine on the Superconscious explore this difference.

When Psychoanalysis and Psychosynthesis are compared, the role of Freud's Superego, with its conscience, is often identified with the role played by guidance from the Superconscious. This confuses two very different levels of consciousness. According to Assagioli the Superego is: "To a great extent introjected from parental prohibitions and commands. This type of conscience is on the level of the personality." (1975, p. 232) The Superego is very often driven by fear, "but the experience of the Superconscious reality does away with fear… In the calm atmosphere of the Superconscious, however, such feelings (fear, aggression, hatred) cannot exist." (2007, p. 25) (My brackets)

The Superconscious remains unconscious only for as long as it remains unexplored. Once we consciously seek to connect with it, it becomes just as available to us as the Lower and Middle Unconscious. It is important to remember that superconscious energies can be repressed. This happens when the self is too identified with personal needs and values.

We need to distinguish between the *pre-rational* union of mother and child that occurs in the Lower Unconscious, and the *trans-rational* union with superconscious energies. These are often confused, and seen as equally spiritual experiences. But there is a difference. The child is dependent, ego-centric and solely focused on its own needs. What characterizes spirituality however, is the ability to care for someone or something other than ourselves and our loved ones.

Transpersonal energies inform a universal ethic. They open up to the universal whilst retaining individual cognitive structures and values. A child is obviously not bad for being ego-centric; this is natural at this stage of our development. We should also keep in mind the difference between the crowd consciousness that an enthusiastic fan might feel during a football match (ethno-centric), and the unitive consciousness we can experience in group meditation, when we feel at one with humanity (world-centric).

THE COLLECTIVE UNCONSCIOUS

The Collective Unconscious (4), which is ranging from the Lower Unconscious to the Superconscious, represents our surrounding psychological environment within. We are in constant telepathic contact with the world outside ourselves and are influenced by everything humanity has experienced and is experiencing. Through psychotherapeutic work or in meditation, we may discover that what we believed to be energies of our personal consciousness, were in fact collective energies. For example, we can identify certain behaviour and personality traits that have been in our family for generations. We may also find that thoughts and feelings in our social environment impact us from afar. Love, hate, fear and trust are impersonal energies flowing among us, yet in many ways we give them a personal flavour when we identify with them.

THE SELF – A CENTRE OF PURE SELF-AWARENESS AND WILL

We have already discussed 'the self', so I will here only outline a few key points. In the centre (5) of the diagram we find the self or the observer. This is the centre of the personality; the subject, and presence of the observer. The observer is a point of pure self-awareness and will, but around it extends a field of consciousness (6). This is the circular luminous field of awareness where we experience the content of consciousness.

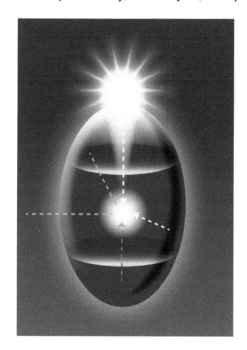

What we think, feel or sense emerges here from the four levels of the unconscious discussed earlier. Intuitions are coming to us directly from the soul (8) (see illustration). Here the observer reflects and interprets all the incoming energies through the psychological functions. Here we recognise and identify what we think, feel and sense at any given time. We can then act on the content or not; if we don't maintain an active focus, it will often disappear. Most of us are identified with the contents of consciousness. We think we are our thoughts and feelings. We have not yet recognized the difference between consciousness *and* its content; that is to say, we have not yet disidentified with the contents of our consciousness. This is a fact anyone can experience by simply trying to observe the content of their consciousness.

Clearly, we are not completely separate from our thoughts and feelings, yet we are something different from them. Reaching this level of insight is the first step towards a personal psychosynthesis. It establishes a stable centre of observation from which we can learn to master the myriad of energies from the personality and the soul. One of Assagioli's key statements is: "We are dominated by everything with which our self becomes identified. We can dominate and control everything

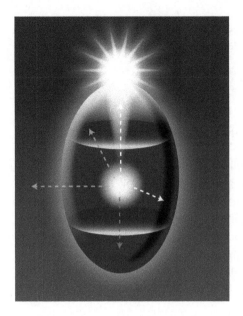

The Egg Diagram and the projection of the Self

from which we disidentify ourselves". When we say "I'm angry," or "I'm sad", we identify with the feeling. If we instead say: "a wave of anger is affecting me", then we distinguish between the feeling and the observer. Then we can decide what we want to do with the feeling and this will give us a sense of ownership and responsibility. The experience of the self as a centre of pure self-awareness and will is psychologically vitally important and should be developed. It enables presence, integrity and, above all, an authentic identity and sense of self.

We should point out that the self can *project* its consciousness into the various levels of the unconscious (see diagram). It is not a passive receiver of impulses; it explores and transforms the energies it encounters. Psychosynthesis offers many methods and techniques of doing this.

EGO, "I" AND THE PERSONALITY

Before moving on to the Transpersonal Self, it may be good to see how some popular ideas in psychology relate to Psychosynthesis. This can help us see how Assagioli's Psychosynthesis represent an entirely new way of thinking. The following is my clarification.

According to Freud and others, the ego can be understood as a structure in the personality that provides a sense of identity organized around rational values. These values usually echo the dominant values of one's culture and society. The ego functions as an 'organizing centre' and the identity the ego provides consist of the social roles with which the individual is identified, the role of mother, wife and or professional occupation. In this sense the ego is something different from Assagioli's self.

The ego can also be defined more broadly as the mind's need to limit and isolate itself through "contraction". It is in the nature of the mind to separate itself from its surroundings. This development is necessary for self-awareness, but it forms a great obstacle for the growth of soul consciousness, where identity is individualised unity. Our ego will remain in control as long as we are identified with the mind.

The ego develops through external norms and values, yet the "I" can be something other than the ego. The I can be a self-conscious identity consisting of a wide range of values and perspectives and in some evolved cases coming from the Superconscious. The I is the identity we create on whatever level of consciousness we inhabit based on the images of self with which we are at any given time identified. If we are identified with our ego, the ego is the I, but if we are in contact with the Superconscious, then the I will be far more individuated, free and humanistic. There are many I's, from body consciousness to soul consciousness. Ken Wilber refers to "the Actual Self" (the "authentic" or healthily-integrated self at any particular stage of development) in his psychology.

The Superego is the collection of moral laws we learned and internalised during childhood. These laws are culturally defined and direct the socialisation of a child. The Superego will remain in control, as long as the individual needs the security and limiting safety it provides.

The personality is the collective expression of the physical body, emotions and mind and everything they contain. The personality only comes into being when we discover we have a will, and able to focus it on deliberately selected target. Until then we are little more than a series of more or less self-conscious roles adapted because of various social circumstances. Personality requires a certain level of development and maturity; because of this, not everyone has one in the technical sense of the word. Assagioli's personal psychosynthesis refers to this integration of the personality.

As can be seen, none of the above definitions are the same as Assagioli's self, the level of pure self-awareness and will in the centre of the personality.

SOUL AND THE TRANSPERSONAL SELF

We are now at the very source of the self and consciousness of man. I prefer to call this source "soul" (8) because it reminds us that we are living divine beings. Assagioli referred to it primarily as "the Transpersonal Self" in the keeping with the scientific approach that was so important to him.

We have already talked about the soul in Chapter I, so let me here elaborate on the key aspects. As mentioned we are not talking about two selves, but consciousness of the self can be experienced at two different levels. On the personal levels we can experience the self as pure self-awareness, but nevertheless feel separated from the people around us. In the world of the Superconscious our experience of self can expand immensely, and we can become part of a unified consciousness without losing our individual purpose.

Thousands of people have described how they through meditation or spontaneous experiences have entered an identity far greater than their usual limited self-awareness. This consciousness is not limited by any personal identity; it is an impersonal being, it is universal and represents the essence of all human beings.

It is important to emphasize that Assagioli refers to the soul as a living being, and that he has a theistic approach to spirituality. When we experience connection to soul, we are "participating in some way in the divine nature". (1975, p. 44)

Assagioli frequently refers to Christianity and Hinduism. He quotes St. Augustine: "When the soul loves something it becomes like unto it; if it should love terrestrial things it becomes terrestrial, but if it should love God (we may ask) does it not become God?" (1975, p. 44) He also emphasized the duality between the personal self and the soul, and between the soul and the universal Self (God). He warned against confusing the various levels of self-awareness, that is, to believe one is God or the soul before one has realized and demonstrated this level of consciousness. This is the same as confusing an acorn with an oak tree. Potential is not the same as a fully realized truth.

Assagioli places the Transpersonal Self at the top of the Egg Diagram to show the direction of the journey and the expansion of consciousness necessary to merge the personal with the transpersonal. Assagioli writes: "The disregard of this vital distinction leads to absurd and dangerous consequences." (1975, p. 45) This is the danger of ego inflation. From this perspective removing the star from the top of the diagram, as some writers have done, is not appropriate.[8]

Soul connects with the self via the illuminated channel that functions as a bridge between the two levels of consciousness (7). The soul creates the Bridge of Consciousness by projecting part of its consciousness into the world of the personality. Assagioli writes: "The ego or the conscious "I", is an emanation or projection of the Self." (1967b) This is an example of evolutionary Panentheism, for as the soul is an emanation (outflow) of the Universal Self (God), so is the personal self.

This link has also been called the silent path, because it is in silence that higher

---

8   This topic is being explored in depth in (Sørensen, 2008)

levels of consciousness are contacted and recognized. In this sense, we can say that the soul's higher consciousness is reflected in the brain. It remains a pale reflection until the spiritual process begins, and the soul increasingly manifests itself through the brain and the physical nervous system. We do not experience consciousness as located in some particular spot in the brain. We experience consciousness through the mind and the mind is not limited to the physical body.

Imagine a luminous presence just above your head, an image familiar to Eastern Spiritual writings. This is the true man, the immortal soul seeking to manifest the Superconscious through the forces of the Middle and Lower Unconscious. Here the personal self facilitates the collaboration between the soul and the Lower and Middle Unconscious.

When the soul is fully manifested in the personality the duality between the soul and the self vanishes as does the limited personal self. Several stages mark this development; at the end the enlightened man steps forward. Assagioli gives examples of many of the enlightened ones who have achieved this level of development: "Gandhi, Florence Nightingale, Martin Luther King, Albert Schweitzer". (1974, p. 122)

There's no essential difference between the consciousness of the soul and the self. An analogy Assagioli used (Undated 2) to describe this is the relationship between the sun and its reflection in a mirror. The sunlight in the mirror has the same qualities as its source; it lights and heats. Yet, if we see only the reflection and not the source, we might think that the mirror itself creates its light. The same applies to the moon: it only reflects the light from the sun. This is also the case with the self if we forget its link to the soul. Here meditation can lead us to the source.

The soul's energies penetrate the entire Egg. Children frequently experience superconscious energies, but this doesn't mean that the soul is located at the bottom of the Egg Diagram, just as the sun is not on the ground even if its light reaches the earth.

The crucial difference between the soul and the self is in the level of intensity and expansion of consciousness. The level of soul is higher than our mental states and the soul is fully conscious of its unity with other souls and the world soul. The star at the top of the chart (8) relates to what the East calls "the Jewel in the Lotus." This represents the core of the soul. (Assagioli, 2007, p. 90)

This core is the stable, unmovable witness; our inner observer which is outside time and space in the eternal present, fully awake and conscious of its cosmic nature. If the self is a 100 watt light bulb emanating from the centre of the brain, then the soul is a 1,000,000 watt bulb shining in eternity.

When the little light in the brain shines with the same intensity as the light in "heaven", we have reached enlightenment. The energies and potentialities in the Superconscious are creative forces radiating from the soul: wisdom, love, beauty and so on. (1974, p. 119) In the same way the self at the level of personality radiates thoughts, emotions and physical actions.

The soul is open to Universal or Cosmic Consciousness. This is why Assagioli placed the star partly within the Egg Diagram and partly without. This tells us that the soul's consciousness points in two directions: towards the individual and towards the Universal Self. At the level of the soul, the soul is an expression of unified consciousness because it is identified with the whole, yet it also has an individual purpose. This purpose is an expression of the transpersonal will; it is the "soul's calling", and represents the journey it takes, both alone and together with other souls. The soul acquires experience through its choices, and ultimately, wisdom. At the level of the soul the soul is wise and good, but when it is manifest in the body, it cannot bring these qualities to the personality before it has developed the ability to express love and wisdom at this level.

The soul represents the level of consciousness open to the universal. But it also has a will-to-be-Self and expresses this will through its unique identity. In this way the soul can become a unique self, retaining its individuality in spite of its universality. Assagioli quotes Radhakrishnan:

"The peculiar privilege of the human self is that he can consciously join and work for the whole and embody in his own life the purpose of the whole. The two elements of selfhood: Uniqueness (each-ness) and universality (all-ness) grow together until at last the most unique becomes the most universal." (1974, p. 128)

Let this be the last word on the soul for now. Admittedly, these perspectives are not easy to communicate or understand; basically the soul cannot be grasped by the intellect, only experienced. We will return to the soul in Chapter X and establish how we can work with the soul in practice.

ASSAGIOLI'S' OTHER MODEL OF THE PERSONALITY

Assagioli developed ideas for other models of the personality in his writing, which are a supplement to the Egg Diagram. These models can be very useful when trying to understand the different aspects of Psychosynthesis. One of the symbols he used to describe the relationship between the soul and the personality is:

The soul's illumination of the personality

"Abstract geometrical symbols are often combined with the symbol of the sun or a star; e.g., the visualization of an equilateral triangle which symbolizes the three aspects of the personality – physical, emotional and mental – and above the apex of the triangle a sun or a star, with radiating rays, symbolizing the Self. This is a very apt symbol to illustrate the process towards and the achievement of spiritual psychosynthesis through the action of, the pervasion by, the spiritual Self of the reconstructed or renewed personality." (1975, p. 203)

In my diagram *The soul's illumination of the personality,* which I have created to illustrate this idea, we see the equilateral triangle representing the integrated personality. That is, the energies from the Lower and Middle Unconscious are gathered around the self. This integration is our personal psychosynthesis. As mentioned, the three basic aspects of personality are the body, emotions, and the mind.

In the middle of the triangle I have added the self – as a point of pure self-awareness and will. Above the triangle we have the sun as a symbol of the soul. It wants to pervade the personality with its rays, that is, with the contents of the Superconscious, in order to induce a spiritual psychosynthesis. At this stage the soul and the personality are united and we can manifest superconscious energies through the body, emotions and thoughts.

The dotted line between the self and the soul is the Bridge of Consciousness, which gradually develops its capacity to transmit the consciousness of the soul into the personality. Here I have combined the known elements from the Egg Diagram in order to illustrate that development is a movement from the bottom to the top assisted by the self and from the top to the bottom directed by the soul.

Assagioli illustrates this idea in this way:

"The spiritual elements that come down like rays of sunlight into the human personality- into our personal consciousness- and form a link between our ordinary human personality and the Higher Self, the spiritual Reality. They are like rays of light pouring down, taking on various shades of colour and dispersing, depending on the permeability or the transparency of our personal consciousness." (2007, p. 241)

In the next chapter we will look at how the personality becomes permeable to superconscious energies, which is part of the journey of self-development. In order to illustrate the personal self's journey from self to soul consciousness, we must immerse ourselves in Psychosynthesis' theory of development.

CHAPTER III

THE DEVELOPMENTAL THEORY
OF PSYCHOSYNTHESIS

*"Maslow has presented an illuminating progression of
five stages of evolutionary development."* (Assagioli)

In the last chapter, I quoted Assagioli's remark that the Egg Diagram, "leaves out its dynamic aspect, which is the most important and essential one".

This dynamic aspect is The Developmental Theory of Psychosynthesis. In *Psychosynthesis*, Assagioli gives a brief outline of this, and he later expands on the idea in *The Act of Will*. The theory illustrates the self's journey from preconscious, to self-conscious, to superconscious awareness. Here I will present a general outline of this process.

Assagioli was inspired by the Italian poet and writer Dante Alighieri (1265-1321). He considered Dante an enlightened being, and he compares the process of psychosynthesis to Dante's Divine Comedy, which he describes as "a wonderful picture of a complete psychosynthesis." (1975, p. 211) Dante's poem is about the soul's journey from hell, through purgatory and into paradise. As Assagioli writes:

"The first part, the Pilgrimage through Hell- indicates the analytical exploration of the Lower Unconscious. The second part – the Ascent of the Mountain of Purgatory- indicates the process of moral purification and gradual rising of the level of consciousness through the use of active techniques. The third part- the visit to Paradise or Heaven- depicts in an unsurpassed way the various stages of superconscious realizations, up to the final version of the Universal Spirit, of God Himself, in which Love and Will are fused."(1975, p. 211)

In this quote, Assagioli describes a model of development moving through several *stages*. Starting at the bottom of the Egg Diagram, it passes through several levels and stages to *Self-realization*. In my Master Dissertation *Integral Psychosynthesis* (Sørensen, 2008), I provide many sources supporting this view. Here I will examine the many nuances that accompany this model.

As Assagioli developed his model, he integrated ideas from many of his colleagues. An important influence was the American psychologist Abraham Maslow. Maslow wrote a number of influential books in the 50s and 60s and was instrumental in the development of Humanistic and Transpersonal Psychology. He is especially known for his "Hierarchy of Needs." Assagioli frequently refers to Maslow in his work and he encouraged his students to study his books. (Undated 2)

In the *The Act of Will*, Assagioli brings Maslow's Hierarchy of Needs into the Egg Diagram. (1974, ch. 8-10) The similarities between Assagioli's and Maslow's ideas are evident and Assagioli quotes Maslow 25 times throughout the book. The integration of Maslow's developmental theory with Assagioli's "static" model is obviously an important point, because it relates his own model with a very clear and dynamic stage model. The evolving self's journey goes through *natural unfolding stages* from the lower unconscious, through the middle unconscious and to the Superconscious and beyond.

There is some confusion about this stage model within the Psychosynthesis milieu. Influential Psychosynthesis thinkers such as John Firman and Ann Gila have suggested extensive changes to Assagioli's original model. We currently find two different theories of development within transpersonal psychology, with Assagioli belonging to the same camp as Maslow and the contemporary American thinker, Ken Wilber. As I discuss this in my MA thesis, I will not dwell on it here, although I will mention an excellent article about the subject by the Dutch thinker Frank Visser. (Visser, 1998)

DEVELOPMENT THROUGH THE THREE LEVELS OF THE UNCONSCIOUS

Let us look at how Assagioli integrates Maslow's ideas into his diagram. As mentioned, Maslow speaks of a 'Hierarchy of Needs', a ladder of necessities that motivate the self. These range from "deficiency needs" like hunger, to higher "being" or "meta- needs" for meaning and enlightenment. Maslow recognised that when needs at one level are met, higher needs will appear, driving the self towards the next level of development. In the next diagram, Maslow's "Hierarchy of Needs" is included in the Egg Diagram from Assagioli's guidelines in *The Act of Will*. (1974, p. 99, 106, 110)

As Assagioli explains:

"Maslow has clearly described the "Hierarchy of Needs" in Motivation and Personality. He speaks first of the basic psychological needs; then of the personal needs

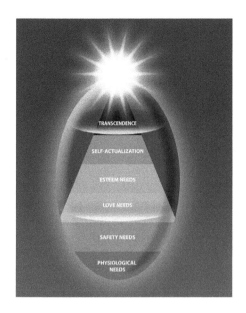

The Egg Diagram and Maslow's Hierarchy of Needs

such as belonging and love, esteem, and self-actualization; and also of a third group: Transpersonal or Metaneeds. Achieving the satisfaction of the first two groups of needs often engenders, paradoxically, a sense of boredom, ennui, emptiness, and meaninglessness. It leads to a more or less blind search for "something other," something more". (1974, p. 106)

Assagioli also explains how Maslow's "Hierarchy of Needs" fits into the Egg Diagram:

"We can look at the diagram of the psychological constitution of man (Egg Diagram). The basic and normal personal needs concern the lower and middle psychological life, both conscious and unconscious. However, there is also a third and higher level – the area of the Superconscious, which culminates in the Transpersonal Self." (1974, p. 110)

So for Assagioli, basic needs such as hunger and security are located in the Lower Unconscious. We can see this from the first quote, where he calls the need for belonging, love, self-esteem and self-actualization personal needs. They are related to the Middle Unconscious, with the need for meaning and transcendence within the Superconscious.

Here Assagioli explains how by satisfying the needs of the Middle Unconscious we activate and develop the *will*:

"All needs evoke corresponding drive toward their satisfaction. The drives concerning the basic elementary needs are more or less blind, instinctive and unconscious. But for the more personal needs the drives gradually lead to conscious volitional acts, aiming at their satisfaction. Therefore every need arouse, sooner or later, a corresponding will." (1974, p. 111)

The development of the Middle Unconscious culminates in what Assagioli calls *personal* psychosynthesis. This is the harmonious integration of the resources in the Lower and Middle Unconscious around the self as a centre of self-awareness and will. He equates this stage of development with Maslow's self-actualization.

(1974, p. 121) Here we find the liberated, goal oriented and self-conscious man, who is fulfilling his personal needs and dreams.

Self-actualization is not primarily driven by the need for recognition (self-esteem). It is by definition "beyond" self-esteem. It is aimed at actualizing creative needs and potentials. At this stage we ask: "How much can I accomplish in life when I focus all my resources on a few selected goals?" We do not have a real conscious will until we reach this type of maturity; we cannot self-actualise at an earlier developmental stage. At this point we draw on holistic energies, integrating the personality's many varied resources in order to achieve an overall goal. We can call this the *integral stage*. The presence of any spiritual or humanitarian motivation is not necessarily suggested at this stage; the self-actualized human can still be selfish. It is very often the urge to be "successful" or to display personal strength and power which drives this stage.

Self-realization begins when the self opens up to superconscious energies. This is often preceded by an existential crisis. According to Assagioli: "When the first two groups of needs are met, they cause, paradoxically, a feeling of boredom, ennui, emptiness and meaninglessness."(1974, p. 106) During this crisis of meaning and purpose whatever stage the Self has reached will determine whether the needs of the soul or the personality will direct our life. If the self reaches a new stage in its development, a new motivation, anchored in the Superconscious, can begin to guide our lives.

EIGHT DEVELOPMENTAL STAGES

Assagioli's model of development distinguishes between a personal and transpersonal psychosynthesis (1975, p. 30) and argues that transpersonal development leads to Self-realization. He defines this as "the blending of the I-Consciousness with the Spiritual Self." (1975, p. 202)

In *The Act of Will*, Assagioli integrates Maslow's theory into this process and presents all the stages of development in connection with the egg-diagram. For him, "Maslow has presented an illuminating progression of five stages of evolutionary development." (1974, p. 120) These stages exemplify different types of people and what motivates them.

The first two types are motivated primarily by the deficiency needs of the Lower Unconscious and Middle Unconscious. The next two are centred on the drive to self-actualize and the higher energies of the Middle Unconscious. Assagioli sees two types of self-actualization, a "selfish" self-actualization and a higher stage actualization, motivated by transpersonal values. The fifth type is the Self-realized person, whose focus is on the creative expression of the energies of the Superconscious and an identification with the soul.

Assagioli sub-divides the fifth stage into three parts, so the path of Self-realization goes through eight stages in total. For him the fifth stage is made up of:

1. *The activation and expression of the potentialities in the Higher Unconscious.* Leonardo da Vinci and Goethe are examples of individuals who reached this stage.

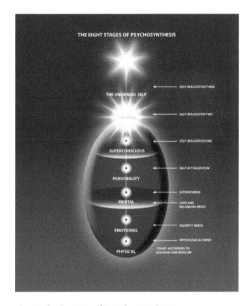

2. *The direct awareness of the Self in the union of the consciousness of the Personal self with the Higher Self.* For Assagioli Gandhi, Florence Nightingale, Martin Luther King and Albert Schweitzer reached this stage.

3. *The communion of the Higher Self with the Universal Self.* The highest mystics of all times belong here.

The Eight Stages of Psychosynthesis

In this diagram all the stages are related to the Egg-Diagram.

Self-realization in its technical meaning is a process, which primarily reaches through the Superconscious, towards the soul and the Universal Self. A prolonged phase of purification is also a part of this process, so the descent into the abyss of the lower unconscious is also necessary. Our personal energies must be purified so they can express the universal love-wisdom that flows from the Superconscious. Dante's journey through Mount Purgatory is a poetic expression of this process.

By responding to the call of the soul, the self can transcend the limitations of "normal consciousness" and manifest the energies needed for Self-realization. Along with the psycho-spiritual path to self- development, other avenues to transcendence relating to different personality types also exist. For Assagioli these include:

1. *Transcendence through Transpersonal Love.* Through altruism, devotion to nature, humanity and the divine, we evolve through the expression of transpersonal love. This way to Self-realization can be called the Way of Love.

   Transcendence through Transpersonal Action. Because humanitarian and socially conscious action can involve personal sacrifice and risk, it can be transpersonal. We can call this the Way of Action.

2. *Transcendence through Beauty.* This is the aesthetic Way. The true artist is willing to endure much pain and suffering in order to express the beauty he or she experiences.

   Transcendence through Self-Realization. This is the way of Enlightenment and concerns those who consciously seek to realize the potentials of the Superconscious and which have their origin in the soul.

We can see these *Ways* of transcendence as forms of will: a fundamental will to transcend the limitations of the personality through the union with someone or something greater. All of the Ways represents the union of love and will. (1974, p. 116)

NON-LINEAR DEVELOPMENT

Maslow's hierarchy of needs might suggest that people develop linearly, but Assagioli, like Maslow, knew this was not the case. Transpersonal qualities can appear in a poorly integrated personality. There are idealists who do not have the strength to realise their ideals, and people sensitive to beauty but ineffective in life. (1974, p. 121)

The development moves through stages, but not necessarily step by step, like walking up stairs. For the gains to be integrated one must take "two steps forward and one step back". When a new, higher stage is conquered, we must return and integrate the earlier stage from the standpoint of the new perspectives, needs and values. Every step forward triggers conflict with earlier needs. This tension must be resolved, integrated and aligned with the new level. Our awakening to the Superconscious must be reflected in our physical and subconscious behaviour. All aspects of the psyche, including subpersonalities, must be reorganised according to the new reality.

To be able to react subconsciously with love and wisdom in all situations requires

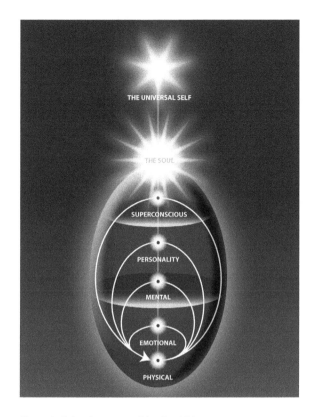

THE UNIVERSAL SELF

THE SOUL

SUPERCONSCIOUS

PERSONALITY

MENTAL

EMOTIONAL

PHYSICAL

The spiral development of the Oval Diagram

a deeply transformative process. Those who practice a spiritual life know this. There is a natural rhythm to the evolutionary process, a flow between ascent and descent, and a gradual conscious collaboration between the self, the soul, and the unconscious parts.

This diagram illustrates this development. It includes the three aspects of the personality – Mental, Emotional and Physical – and the stage of the integrated personality. In a healthy development, a continuous exchange of higher and lower energies takes place, in which our new values inform our sexuality and relationship to money and power. Destructive shadow material may emerge if lower energies are excluded from our spiritual development, a consequence that may be observed within spiritual milieus that focus too much on transcendence.

Superconscious energies must manifest *through the Lower Unconscious* before they can be expressed at the physical level, in service to humanity. Transcending our personal needs is not sufficient; energies from the Lower Unconscious – sexuality, aggression, assertiveness – must be brought in under the domain of the soul's love and wisdom.

Assagioli believed that the aim of enlightenment is to be of service to humanity; the ecstasy we feel at our contact with the soul must serve this purpose. (1975, p. 207, 210, 2006, p. 251, 270) The synthesis of humanity- and ultimately the cosmos – is the goal of evolution.

Evolutionary Panentheism shares this perspective. Transcendental consciousness is of little use unless it can help the struggles of humanity. We are humanity. To use a metaphor: We go up the mountain, as it were (the Superconscious), so we can return to share our inspiration, love and will, knowing that humanity, the earth and cosmos exist together in a divine union. This is a reality on the spiritual level, but not yet on the physical.

Assagioli recognized that different people reach different evolutionary stages at different times. It was important, he argued, to identify a child's evolutionary level in his or her educational setting. (1960) He was also aware of the resistance to such an attitude:

"Another reason or pseudo-reason for the hostility... is a false concept of the equality of human beings and the democratic ideal... It seems...almost an insult to admit that there are people of a higher stature, psychologically and spiritually." (Besmer, 1973)

According to the evolutionary perspective, we have all equal value as human beings, but our perspectives are not equally good. "Gender equality" is a more valuable perspective than male chauvinism or assertive feminism because it is concerned with the total welfare of humanity rather than that of a single sex. There is wider and deeper love in a desire for equality, and people who are driven by this value display a higher level of consciousness in this area.

Another way of illustrating these levels is through the idea of "holarchies". As shown in the diagram these are wholes within wholes, where the body (1) is enclosed by emotions, the emotions (2) by thoughts (3), thoughts by the personality (4), and the personality by the soul (5). The Superconscious is also enclosed by the soul, and finally we have the universal Self (God) enclosing all. Spirit can be experienced both as a universal being (the blue field) and as a universal Self (a core).

DEVELOPMENTAL LINES IN PSYCHOSYNTHESIS

So far we have described the developmental stages of the self and the different needs with which the self identifies from the Preconscious to the Superconscious. Psychosynthesis theory also involves seven psychological functions, through which we experience and expresses the self. This allows for a much more nuanced and varied developmental theory, with each of the functions having their own unique developmental sequence.

The Oval Diagram and Holarchies

The Swiss psychiatrist C.G. Jung spoke of four functions: feeling, thinking, sensing, and intuition. Assagioli included seven in his version. In *The Act of Will*, Assagioli explains the Psychological Functions using the Star Diagram. (1974, p. 13) We can think of the psychological functions as "abilities" we use during our journey through life. The self and the will form the centre of the star out of which the psychological functions emanate, and through which they receive and transmit various energies.

As the diagram shows, Psychosynthesis works with:

Will (7)	Intuition (6)	Thought (5)	Imagination (4)
Desire (3)	Feeling (2)	Sensation (1)	

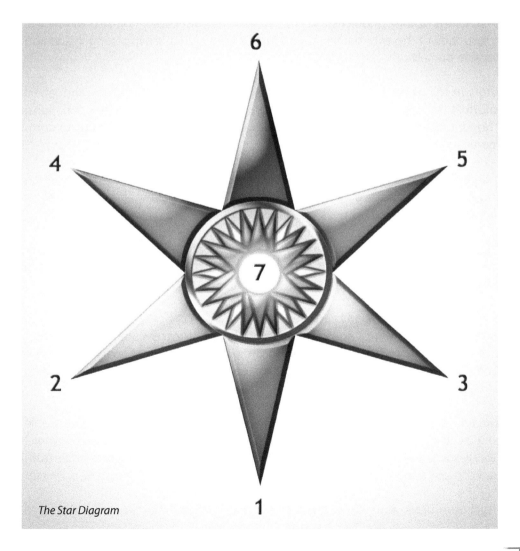

The Star Diagram

We all share these psychological functions; through them we learn to master our lives. They are instruments of action through which the self manifests in the world and seeks to understand the inner and outer worlds. At the centre of the star is the observer, the silent awareness and being, the "Unmoved Mover," in Aristotle's words. From this silent centre active forces emanate *through* the psychological functions, and manifest the current level of consciousness and intention of the self.

The *will* directs our energy through our intentions, choices and decisions. The will is the basic motivation setting everything else in motion, but we rarely notice it. Only with real self-awareness does the will become a *true* will and not simply unconscious desire. We make decisions with our will and our actions reveal our identifications.

Feeling represents our sensitivity, our ability to sense and identify the *quality* of our psychological surroundings. It tells us what feels comfortable or uncomfortable. It responds to the external world and lets us know what is happening inside and outside ourselves.

Thought tell us what something is. It collects, organizes, categorizes and labels information, enabling us to assess impressions coming from other functions. Thought interprets our reality based on our knowledge and enables us to communicate with others through language.

Imagination is the ability to create highly evocative images. We use imagination to visualize reality as it *could* be. Such images influence our emotional and mental life, and so are as "real" as physical, "factual" reality.

Desire includes our instincts, drives, wishes, needs, attractions and repulsions. Desire moves us and makes things happen. There are many levels of desire, from the survival instinct to the passionate love of God.

Sensation involves the body and the senses. It enables the self to act in the physical world. The body anchors energies coming from the other psychological functions, and informs us of what is happening in the outside world and how it affects our body. Sensation and the body provide the energy and life force required to keep us healthy.

Intuition is mainly a transpersonal function, according to Assagioli, but is available to us at all levels of consciousness. Intuition provides a direct insight into the whole, how we or a situation fits into the bigger picture. It provides direct access to the truth and conveys a sense of the interconnection of everything throughout the universe.

Psychosynthesis aims to develop these psychological functions. As Assagioli writes, Psychosynthesis promotes "the development of the aspects of the personality which are either insufficient or inadequate." (1975, p. 29) Assagioli was concerned with "unbalanced development" and many of his techniques are aimed at strengthening the weaker psychological functions. (1975, p. 57)

In *The Act of Will* Assagioli argues that the psychological functions develop hierarchically[9]; they can be weak or more highly evolved. In Maslow's hierarchy the needs at the top of the pyramid are more complex, and represent a higher development than the basic needs further down. Assagioli does the same with the psychological functions: "The existence of different levels having different values is an evident and undeniable manifestation of the great law of evolution, as it progresses from simple and crude levels to more sophisticated and highly organized ones." (1974, p. 99) Applying this to love Assagioli's writes that "a love that is overpowering, possessive, jealous and blind is at a lower level than one that is tender and concerned with the person of the loved one... ". (1974, p. 99)

THE UNIVERSAL SELF

THE SOUL

The same applies to the other psychological functions. The developmental lines illustrate this law as they unfold from the bottom of the Egg Diagram up to the level of the soul. The psychological functions develop towards universality, with higher levels more inclusive than lower ones. Assagioli is aware that hierarchical ideas are not popular. On this he echoes C.G. Jung: "Jung rightly deplores this pseudo-humanitarian concept and false conception of democracy:" The desire to bring all people to the same level and reduce them to the status of sheep by suppressing the natural aristocratic and hierarchical structure (in

---

9   Assagioli supports Maslow and Wilber's notion that the structure of reality is hierarchical or holarchical. His use of Maslow's Hierarchy of Needs is a clear example. He is referring to hierarchies several places in his work: 2007, s.173, 190, 192, 210, Keen 1975.

the psycho-spiritual sense, be it well noted) leads inevitably, sooner or later, to a catastrophe." (1967b)

With the self's own development we have eight fundamental developmental lines. These do not develop equally, which illustrates the complex character of our development and shows why it does not proceed in a linear ladder-like way.

Ken Wilber has done a wonderful job illuminating this subject and the reader seeking a detailed study of these different stages and lines of development can find it in his book *Integral Psychology*.

For example, we can be highly developed cognitively, but less developed emotionally, or we may find it difficult to turn our ideas into action. The eight lines of the Egg Diagram relate directly to the development of the self, but other developmental lines represent various combinations of all the functions. Values, sexuality, aesthetics have their own development, but space does not allow me to discuss this here.

In the diagram, we see a person's self-line (5) developed to the level of rational self-awareness. His empathy, compassion (2) and idealism (7) are also highly developed. If his self-line reaches into the level of the Superconscious, his experience of separateness from other people will dissolve. Our idealism may be highly developed – we may work for the welfare of animals or the rain forest – but our sense of self may not yet reach the level of unity consciousness.

Let me briefly describe the developmental lines of the self and three of the psychological functions.

The developmental line of the *self* (5) expresses the level of consciousness (breadth and height) within and outside the Egg Diagram. It determines our centre of gravity and on what stage we have our anchor of identification, how much we can observe and include of reality from body- to superconscious awareness. Through meditation the self awakens to an enormous inner landscape of energies. Awareness meditation, which involves disidentification from the content of consciousness, is an important tool in this development.

The *will* develops by making deliberate, conscious decisions. Before this, we are driven by instincts, security and adaptation needs. At the personal level the will is oriented towards success and the power to control one's life. When motivated by the good will of the Superconscious we develop the skill to create harmony and synthesis in the world. We can gather people, organizations and nations around charitable and humanistic values that unite the world.

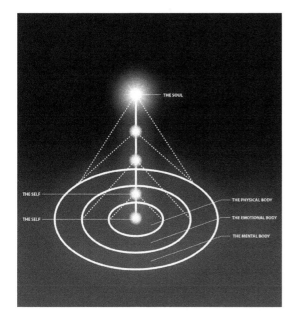

By strengthening the *feeling* function we develop our sensitivity, empathy and the space and strength needed to emotionally contain the world around us. Here we develop our understanding, both horizontally in becoming more inclusive of other people, but also vertically by lifting our feelings to the level of the Superconscious where they can express impersonal, universal and unconditional love. Emotional development provides the strength and inner space needed to contain destructive, heavy and painful emotions.

Thinking relates to our level of understanding and the different perspectives from which we are able to perceive reality. This includes understanding our external social context – our family and the world community – as well as the cultural values that shape our consciousness. "Vertically" this means broadening our perspectives to understand our place in the cosmos and the ocean of energy of which we are a part. This relates to the quality of our interpretations of reality, how integral we are and how many perspectives we include in our awareness of it.

In *A Psychology with a Soul*, Jean Hardy offers an alternative model of development, which is also hierarchical. For her the self develops through the stages of "body", "feelings", "thought" and finally "soul" (see illustration). This shows how multifaceted the development theory of Psychosynthesis has become.

One element of our theory of development remains to be discussed: our relation to the Collective Unconscious, the area outside the Egg Diagram which we share with all of humanity and creation.

THE COLLECTIVE UNCONSCIOUS

The Collective Unconscious consists of different ontological levels of reality and frequencies of energy that we share with all creation. According to this theory, the various levels of consciousness are not created by repressions as some thinkers

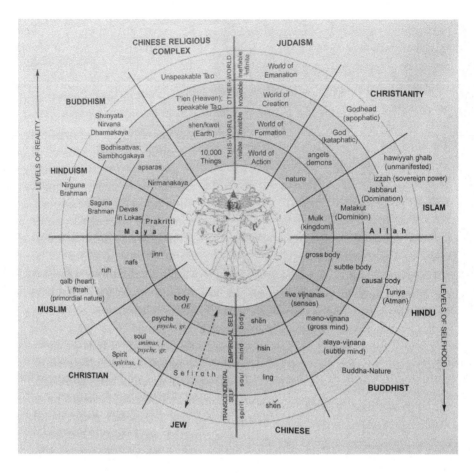

suggest, although we may repress our conscious access to it. Assagioli speaks of what the great scholar Huston Smith (1976), calls "the Great Chain of Being". They are "the various levels of reality or energy fields" which for Assagioli forms "an essential part of Psychosynthesis." (Undated 2)

The majority of the spiritual traditions (Smith, 1976) embrace a hierarchical or holarchical structure of existence. In the diagram,[10] we see how this reality has been recognized by the great mystics and seers of the majority of the world religions.

This idea is also part of the perennial philosophy, which views each of the world's religious traditions as sharing a single, universal truth. Ken Wilber refers to a number of contemporary thinkers who share the same perspective.

---

10 The Great Chain in various Wisdom Traditions, compiled by Huston Smith (graphic layout courtesy of Brad Reynolds).

The Great Chain of Being came into existence with the creation of the cosmos. This posits not only a material world – which may have come about through a Big Bang – but also a number of inner worlds created through the involution of the spirit, mentioned in Chapter I. Assagioli shares this view and he writes (2007, p. 84):

"The third group of symbols, a frequently occurring one, is that of elevation, ascent or conquest of the 'inner space' in an ascending sense. There are a series of inner worlds, each with its own special characteristics, and within each of them there are higher levels and lower levels. Thus in the first of these, the world of passions and feelings, there is a great distance, a marked disparity of level, between blind passion and the highest feelings. Then there is the world of intelligence, or the mind. Here too are different levels: the level of the concrete analytical mind, and the level of higher, philosophical reason (nous). There is also the world of the imagination, a lower variety and a higher variety, the world of intuition, the world of the will, and higher still, those indescribable worlds which can only be referred to by the term 'worlds of transcendence'".

The diagram below provides a basic outline of these inner worlds. My article *Psychosynthesis and Panentheism* (Sørensen, 2015), includes many quotes from Assagioli relevant to this discussion. The diagram shows various hierarchies or holarchies where higher worlds transcend and include lower worlds, and can also be seen as a model of Jung's Collective Unconscious. As Assagioli remarks: "The collective unconscious is a vast world stretching from the biological to the spiritual level, in which therefore distinctions of origin, nature, quality and value must be made." (1967b)

The diagram on the next page illustrates how the self, with the rest of humanity, must journey through the different worlds to return to its spiritual source. This journey begins with the unification of the self and the soul, and continues with the Universal Self. The imagination is a synthesising function, which operates on several levels simultaneously: sensation, feeling, thinking and intuition. (1975, p. 143)

"THE GREAT CHAIN OF BEING"

This concludes my survey of the theory of development. My description of the different stages has been necessarily brief; the reader is encouraged to pursue the references given in this chapter.

We now turn to the seven core concepts in Psychosynthesis, beginning with disidentification, but let us conclude with a striking appeal from Assagioli.

"I make a cordial appeal to all therapists, psychologists and educators to actively engage in the needed work of research, experimentation and application. Let us feel and obey the urge aroused by the great need of healing the serious ills which at present are affecting humanity; let us realize the contribution we can make to the creation of a new civilization characterized by an harmonious integration and cooperation, pervaded by the spirit of synthesis." (Assagioli, 1975, p. 9)

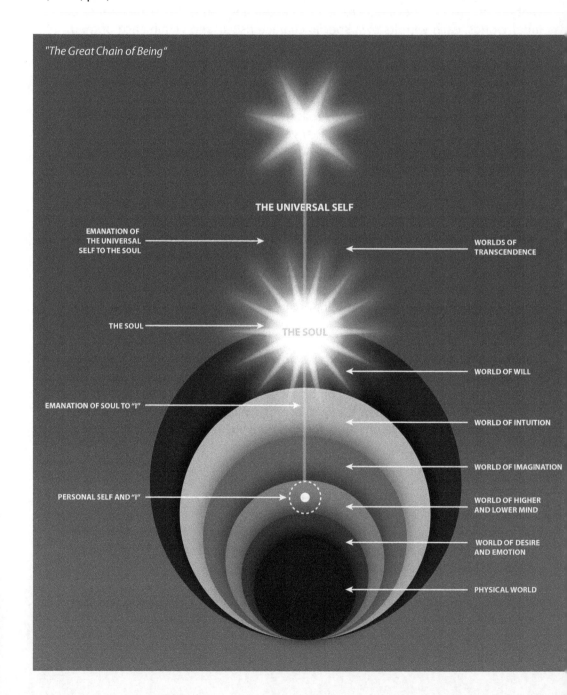

CHAPTER IV

DISIDENTIFICATION
– THE WAY TO FREEDOM

"The conscious and purposeful use of self-identification-
or disidentification, is basic in Psychosynthesis." (Assagioli)

As mentioned in Chapter I, the aim of disidentification is to stop ourselves from identifying with social roles or certain limiting aspects of our personality. Psychosynthesis is a therapy as well as an individual practice. Our most important tool as therapists is our personality, so we need to look carefully at both these aspects.

Disidentification creates a neutral distance in us from whatever we identify with. For Ken Wilber it is "converting hidden subjects to conscious objects". The observer is not the observed, so whenever we disidentify from false self-images it help us to discover our real self – the observer. Identifying with certain psychological states, social roles and identities allows them to become a distal object or "me". Disidentifying is to let go of the attachment to this "me" by observing it and integrating it in its proper way. It then becomes an object of consciousness. We then discover ourselves as the observer – a point of pure self-awareness and will. This provides more access to our multifaceted nature and potentialities. Disidentification is a way to freedom, because the observer is gradually liberated from the content of consciousness. One of the major goals of psychosynthesis is to train us in this technique, so we can learn to identify with self-awareness rather than thoughts, feelings and the body.

Practicing disidentification we observe the content of our consciousness; our sensations, feelings and thoughts. It can be done anywhere, with eyes closed or open. It is based on introspection and the loving and firm affirmation that we are not the objects of our consciousness. We are the observer and explore how we can contain whatever arises in consciousness without identifying with it. The process ends with an examination of our pure self-awareness. We become conscious about being conscious and from there we can identify with self-awareness itself.

Recognizing ourselves as the observer, we are free to *choose* how to express ourselves. Yet understanding this is not enough. Jettisoning old roles and unconscious conditioning requires discipline and work. The practice is similar to Mindfulness, but in contrast to Buddhism, Psychosynthesis retains the self as a central concept and a reality.

Let us look at how Psychosynthesis Psychotherapy uses disidentification. For Assagioli the purpose of Psychosynthesis is to "release, or let us say, help to release, the energies of the Self. Prior to this, the purpose is to help integrate, to synthesize, the individual around the personal self, and then later to effect the synthesis between the personal ego and the Self." (1975, p. 65)

Here Assagioli describes Psychosynthesis' two central goals, personal and transpersonal psychosynthesis. One integrates the Lower and Middle Unconscious around the self as the observer and will, i.e. "self-actualization." Next step is to liberate the energies from the Superconscious and put them into service for humanity, this will prepare the personality for Self-realization, the fusion of self and soul.

As mentioned, we can access superconscious energies while lacking an integrated personality, i.e. the creative artist whose personal life is a mess. The stages of development serve as a general map helping therapists orient themselves, when guiding a client toward progress.

We must always plan therapy according to the needs of the client. "The emphasis is put on a holistic or integral conception of the treatment" (Assagioli, 1975, p. 66). We must, that is, base our therapeutic interventions on a holistic view of our clients.

Techniques must not be overused. According to Assagioli the "human factor, of the living interpersonal relation between the therapist and the patient" is central (1975, p. 67). But as the will is essential in Psychosynthesis, techniques to self-help are important. Clients' must participate in their psychosynthesis by applying the many active techniques the therapy offers. "The conscious and purposeful use of self-identification- or disidentification," Assagioli writes, "is basic in Psychosynthesis." (1975, p. 111)

Assagioli saw certain stages in therapy. These shouldn't be confused with the overall stages of development, reviewed in Chapter III. It is not unusual to see such a confusion in the Psychosynthesis literature. The therapeutic stages are applied in accordance with a therapeutic process and they needn't be followed in strict succession; they can be adjusted to suit the client's *current developmental stage*. (1975, p. 29)

But the therapeutic stages are applied as part of the overall personal and transpersonal psychosynthesis, and they contain *natural unfolding stages* according to

Maslow's and Dante's suggestions. Assagioli clearly confirms this in the chapter where he describes the therapeutic process.

Psychosynthesis Psychotherapy should help the client to:

1. *Experience herself as a loving* witness who can observe, hold and transform the content of consciousness.

2. *Experience herself as a dynamic observer* aware of the will-to-be-self and through this awareness, actualising chosen needs, resources and values of the observer.

Assagioli describes the therapeutic stages (1975, p. 21) leading to psychosynthesis:

1. Thorough knowledge of one's personality

2. Control of its various elements

3. Realization of one's true Self- the discovery or creation of a unifying centre

4. Psychosynthesis: the formation or reconstruction of the personality around the new centre.

Let's look at these stages and the important part disidentification plays in it.

1. Thorough knowledge of one's personality

Here we explore the unconscious region of the oval diagram, how its resources and limitations relate to the client's current need for healing. Assagioli recommends that we first form an overview of the client's life, how its themes may be linked to family and cultural influences. At this stage we look at what the client is already conscious of.

Investigating the Lower Unconscious too soon can be dangerous. Trauma and repressed material may overwhelm an unprepared client. Assagioli recommends getting an overview of the client, through autobiography, diary and interviews. (1975, p. 101) Personality tests may be useful. The consolidation of a trusting relationship between client and therapist is important at this stage.

We begin the exploration of the unconscious by examining the themes the client brings to therapy, focussing on areas the client has chosen or which seem particularly important to us at this stage. The depth of the exploration depends on the client's wishes, the time and economic means available.

The client should have some experience of the inner observer before proceeding to this stage. At first aided by the therapist but "later, in the course of therapy the attitude can and should be assumed more and more consciously, deliberately and fully." (Assagioli, 1975, p. 69) I will in the next chapter discuss Awareness Based Psychotherapy, which concerns the development of the observer in therapy.

The client is now trained to disidentify from the roles, beliefs and inner voices that emerge in therapy. He sees that he is *not* his body-states, feelings, desires, thoughts, or fantasies, but a loving observer who contains these and slowly learns to master them. At the beginning of treatment Assagioli suggests that the therapist gives the client instructions on the oval diagram. (1975, p. 85) This should be introduced as an hypothesis clients can verify through their own experiences and insights. The goal is for the client to become a loving witness to his everyday psychological processes, and disidentification is the primary method.

2. Control of the Various Elements of the Personality

This stage deals with the repressed material that has now emerged. The four stages are not absolutely separate processes in time, and can often be addressed in the *same* session.

Here the client learns mastery of the limiting and painful influences coming from the unconscious, and which prevent him from being an authentic self, a liberated being actualising its resources, needs and values. If the first step towards freedom is to disidentify; the next is to liberate the self from the inner prison.

Assagioli uses strong language to describe this stage, which may give us pause. He speaks of "dominating" and "controlling" the Lower Unconscious. (1975, p. 22) His description of mastering unconscious inhibitions, taboos and complexes, sounds like a kind of psychological warfare. Let me give a few examples.

"There are certain strong trends, certain vital elements which, however much we may disparage and condemn them, obstinately persist. This is true especially concerning sexual and aggressive drives ". (1975, p. 24) In the chapter proceeding this he does emphasise why we should *not* repress or judge the many impulses. (1975, p. 51, 56)

He also talks about how we should observe unconscious forces and drives with "cold, impersonal observation", in order for us to create a "psychological distance". (1975, p. 23)

His rhetoric is forceful: "It is well known that too much criticism and analysis are apt to paralyze and even kill our emotions and feelings. This critical faculty, which we often employ indiscriminately and harmfully against our higher feelings and creative potentialities, should instead be used to free ourselves from undesirable impulses and tendencies." (1975, p. 23) In my opinion this is not a very useful approach, and seems to differ from Assagioli's general attitude.

Assagioli told Sam Keen: "Self-consciousness involves our being a witness – a pure, objective, loving witness – to what is happening within and without." (Keen, 1974) I chose to start with the wisdom of the loving witness, which relates more to my own experiences and with what I feel was Assagioli's basic approach to psychotherapy.

Assagioli says this about Stage two:

"We are dominated by everything with which our self becomes identified. We can dominate and control everything from which we disidentify ourselves." (1975, p. 22)

Assagioli defines what he means by control: "suppression tends to push the drive back again into the unconscious, whereas control implies neither fear nor condemnation but mastery and regulation. In other words, control allows for expression, but expression in some harmless or useful way. Control ensures a "lull" or the time necessary to proceed with the further task of utilizing the energy of the drive or emotion." (1975, p. 108)

I agree with Assagioli, but in my own work I avoid words like "dominance" and "control." They have unhelpful connotations not useful when working toward the "loving witness". Nevertheless we *can* be dominated by unconscious forces. I propose this paraphrase:

"We are dominated by everything with which our self becomes identified. We can master and direct everything from which we disidentify." Assagioli, we know, spoke of mastering and directing our inner energies. What is said here is in keeping with this. (1975, p. 6, 56)

Disidentification leads to mastery of the unconscious, yet it may be necessary for the client to temporarily identify with a traumatic experience before this is achieved. Purifying and releasing emotional intensity makes disidentifying easier. (1975, p. 102) Other techniques are also helpful during this stage: catharsis, bodily discharge, critical analysis.

Let's look at how our clients can master different psychological influences so they can identify with and freely express their authentic self.

Disidentification helps us understand who we are and how to let go of uncon- scious assumptions limiting our identity. As mentioned, our identity is largely con- structed from aspects of our personality which represent only some of our inner resources. Our identity can be formed by: (1975, p. 112-113)

1. An identification with the psychological functions and social roles

2. The Self as pure self-awareness and will

3. The soul as pure self-awareness and will

Regarding the first type, we can be identified with one or more psychological functions:

Our Body, if we are identified with our looks, skills, or talents related to the body.

Our Feelings, if we are identified with our temperament, i.e. sweet, lively, tough.

Our Intellect, if we are identified with our knowledge, education or attitudes.

Our Social roles as mother, father, woman, man, our career as well as unconscious roles such as victim, clown, good girl, rebel, etc.

These identifications present challenges. They are limited and therefore unstable, and they may have little bearing on reality. Someone identified with his strength often represses the parts of his nature contrary to this. A woman identified as a mother faces an identity crisis when the children leave home. These types of identities can create inner tension when conflicting elements of the personality emerges, something I discuss this further on, when I explore the art of synthesis.

Disidentification involves the letting go of limiting identifications, allowing us to make use of all our personality. If a client says: "I'm not good with relationships," we ask, "what part of you is talking now? "By pointing out that a particular "belief" is speaking, the client can *observe* this "voice" as something quite different from herself. She becomes the loving observer. Through this we are free to look at our self-perceptions so that we can re-evaluate our identity and *consciously choose* new and more suitable identifications.

When we identify with the loving witness disidentification uncovers the self as the observer and will. The loving witness is consciousness itself and not the content of consciousness. Eventually we can identify with the soul, which we will discuss in Chapter X.

When we discover "that which we are not", we can choose new authentic roles and expressions. Yes, we are fathers or mothers, but we must create this role in our own authentic, unique way, just as we must create the other roles we play in life. Finding what is authentic is what the next stage is about.

3. Realization of one's true Self- the discovery or creation of a unifying centre

At this stage the client discovers what is authentic- as we must do ourselves. The discoveries of the previous stages provide a new aim and direction for the therapy. We may want to strengthen the experience of the self and its contact with the soul, or to develop specific sides of ourselves i.e. a talent, a social role, an inner quality. We may want to bolster our courage, confidence, authority, or improve one of the psychological functions.

The aim here is to define our true identity in relation to our life and current stage of development. Above we defined three types of identity. One of them was based on the authentic roles we play in life, and we could call them *the actual self*. Assagioli proposed we can add two more types of identity, what we can call the false and the future self. Let's look at them:

The False self is formed of unconscious or conscious self-perceptions that do not correspond to who we are. Assagioli defines six types of false self-images; (1975, p. 167) they are different types of self-perceptions: when we underestimate or over-estimate ourselves; when we wish we were something we're not; self-perceptions based on projective identification, and others. These appear as subpersonalities – inner "voices" – that direct our behaviour and we will explore them further in Chapter VII.

The Future self is what Assagioli calls The Ideal Model: "a realistic image of what you may be, when you focus your will and enthusiasm to becoming it." We will speak of this in Chapter VI.

The Actual self, let us repeat, represents realistic self-perceptions based on our present level of development. Identifications depending on the roles we play in life. They are temporary and change as we develop. Ideally, we should *know* that our social or professional roles do not define us, and here the role as psychotherapist and teacher should be a good example. Actual selves are authentic because we are *conscious* of them. We freely choose these roles and fulfil them in ways that truly express who we experience ourselves to be. This also applies to the more informal or archetypal roles, such as "diplomat", "helper" or "organizer". Ken Wilber calls this the actual self (the "authentic" or healthily-integrated self at any particular stage of development). It is a stage-self, because it derives its motivation from the different layers of the oval diagram.

The self is the personal self, the observer, and is a reflection or emanation of the soul. Even if limited, it is a true self, and always the same – a centre of pure self-awareness and will. Self-aware but without content, it is permanent and stable. Even though our identification with the soul evolves and becomes individual-universal, the experience of the presence and the dynamic force of "I-amness" is the same through all the stages.

The Soul – The Transpersonal Self. This is the true Self, an eternal indestructible loving and wise witness. The soul guides, protects and strengthens us through its presence and inspiration. Although we have no direct conscious contact with it, the soul remains present in the background of our being.

Disidentification is crucial in our struggle for identity. We must *release self-perceptions based on what we are not.* Disidentification helps uncover false selves. We learn to step back and examine the needs and values of the false self. We question their motivation: are they based on authentic needs or are they based on how other people perceive us?

Disidentification minimizes a dominant role's influence. Some women identify as mothers so much that they neglect themselves, their husband, their work etc., which may lead to conflict. Greater balance is needed so that she can be a mother less obsessively. She can find joy and inspiration in other roles, which will have a positive impact on her children.

There are many ways to disidentify and we will look into these below. With a clear image of what we want to achieve, we move to the next stage.

4. Psychosynthesis: the formation or reconstruction of the personality around the new centre.

Here we realize the Ideal Model, which serves as a centre around which the new personality develops. This can take time, depending on the goal, and usually we work at developing specific areas, such as self-esteem. Several techniques help realize the new identity, visualization, awareness meditation, goal oriented action. Different psychological types have individual needs and we should organise the therapy accordingly. Characteristic of this stage is the will and its power to motivate other psychological functions. An authentic goal stimulates joy and triggers higher needs which provide the energy and motivation to realize it. This brings energy to the will and it is primarily the will-to-be-self that controls this process.

Disidentification plays a large part here, particularly disidentifying from resistance to the process. It is a psychological law that *the future awakens the past*. As we realize a new identity, old ones surface, creating conflict. Manifesting a new identity can produce fatigue and fear due to the resistant false self and lower our energy levels.

Let's look at disidentification in practice.

Assagioli's Disidentification Exercise

As mentioned, disidentification is crucial for Assagioli. We should introduce it, he says, as early as possible, and because we live so much on our "outside" rather than our centre, Assagioli suggests we practice disidentification as a "daily psycho-spiritual health measure". (1975, p. 118)

Assagioli, we know, was inspired by the Eastern practices of Vipassana, Raja yoga, and perhaps by what is known as "the neti neti exercise." This Sanskrit expression means "neither this, nor that." Through it one comes to understand the nature of Brahman, by understanding what he is not. That is, the distinction between consciousness itself and its contents.

Assagioli's version of the disidentification exercise is included in the appendix. Here I will comment on this, and offer my own. The exercise asks us to simply observe our senses, feelings and thoughts, and affirm that while we *have* a body, but we *are not* it. We *have* emotions, but *are not* them. We *have* thoughts, but *are not* them either. We then observe consciousness itself as well as the subject who wills to meditate and affirm that *we are* "a centre of pure self-awareness and will".

When Assagioli suggests the affirmation: "I have a body, but *I am not* my body", he does not mean a rejection of; he recommends us to say: "I treat it well; I seek to keep it in good health, but it is *not* myself". He knows this can meet resistance: "Among some patients, particularly Americans , there is a great deal of resistance to the idea of disidentifying oneself from one's body, feelings and thoughts; and a deep fear of becoming split into different parts by doing so." (1975, p. 122)

Assagioli suggests that we are so identified – obsessed even – with some part of ourselves that it controls us entirely. We have to abandon this identification so we can experience our centre (the observer), which then collects, includes and syn-thesises *all* of what we are. (1975, p. 123) Assagioli was once asked the following question:

I: "Some people do not like the idea of saying "I have a body, but I am not my body" or other content of consciousness. They feel this is a rejection."

RA: "That is one of the many misunderstandings, which are consequences of the central misunderstanding. No rejection at all, but put things in their place. We need bodies here, and we ought to take care of them and appreciate them … At present to many people it is the body that has them. They are slaves of their body. So as a first reaction, perhaps a separating stage is needed psychologically. We may have to go to the other extreme for a little while in order to reach it. And that is true for every kind of possession." (Undated 2)

We should not "separate" and dissociate ourselves from the body, the task is to be a loving witness who appreciates and embraces it with love. We live in the body, it is a temple, but we are not it. Much research into near death and out-of-body experiences suggests that consciousness can exist outside the body. The body changes, cells are replaced, it passes from fatigue to vitality to pain. So much is obvious. We cannot find a permanent centre of freedom, love and being when we identify with the body. My own experience of many years of daily meditation suggests that disidentifying from the body and the other psychological functions is crucial to achieving pure self-awareness.

Our body, feelings and thoughts are instruments for the self and soul (Assagioli, 1975, p. 117). It's through them that we manifest the self and the soul in the world. Our aim is to develop a compassionate relationship to these functions, as a centre of loving and wise will, capable of mastering, directing and using them. (1975, p. 119)

To say as some have, "I have a body but I am more than my body, "seems, to me, to miss the point and obscures the experience of pure self-awareness. It suggests that my identity is both my body *and* any other content of my consciousness. This seems the opposite of Assagioli's intention with disidentification.

Yet, Assagioli's language can imply that we must maintain a cool distance from our body, emotions and thoughts:

"It is an attitude quite similar, even identical, to that of the natural scientist who objectively, patiently and persistently observes the natural phenomena occurring around him." (1975, p. 114) We've seen that Assagioli suggested a "cold, impersonal observation" of our mental images and complexes. Associating disidentification with science and its cold analytical approach may not be attractive for many people and may seem in contrast with the attitude of "the loving witness".

THE DISIDENTIFICATION PROCESS

We've said that the soul is never separated from the personality; it remains immanently present as a guiding and protective factor. The soul lives in the Superconscious, but like the sun its radiance flows throughout the psyche, although we may not be aware of it. The self has the same task at the level of the personality. All the personality's functions and processes must be filled with loving awareness. Here we do not separate from the body, emotions and thoughts, but contain and develop them with a loving, wise consciousness. We can achieve this only from the centre or self, by recognizing that we are quite different from the body, emotions and mind. To love something requires duality and distance, a space between lover and beloved. We fill this space with loving awareness. In this way disidentification creates a centre as well as connectedness.

When I explain disidentification to my students I emphasize Psychosynthesis' aim of becoming loving observers who can master their lives. This means to *observe, contain and be creative* with our psycho-spiritual energies. Disidentification prepares for a new self-identification, so it is important to:

Observe what happens in the body, emotions and mind, knowing that you are not what you are observing. It's a dual awareness; you direct consciousness toward its source and at the objects of consciousness. Such observation illuminates our inner house, its different levels and rooms, which constitute the personality. Observing facilitates *enlightenment through recognition.*

To contain is to unconditionally accept all that we have in our inner house. This type of love comes from the Superconscious and manifest through the heart centre. It is an impersonal, unconditional love, beyond sympathy and antipathy, and it helps to embrace everything we experience, creating a harmonious "climate" in our inner house. To accept does not mean we agree with the feeling; we simply allow it to be until the transformation has changed the content.

Conscious Breathing. Being aware of our breath anchors our attention, preventing us from losing ourselves in different states of consciousness. By consciously breathing through the various states of consciousness – the body, feelings, and thoughts – we energize habits, and make them easier to release. The breath is always here and now, not in the past or future, and this helps us to be present.

Letting go of identifications is crucial, and only an act of will releases us from our habits. If we learn to let go of everything in the moment, rather than cling to the contents of consciousness, we create more space in our inner house. Consciousness will expand spontaneously, and we have more space to be with whatever arises. Gradually we awaken to consciousness itself, that which we are. This is the will-to-be-self, the intention behind the process. We can disidentify anywhere at any time, in an elevator, on the street, or in deep meditation. The result is the same: Loving detachment, which is the freedom to choose new perspectives and ways of being.

To disidentify is to observe, contain, breathe, and let go.

Assagioli emphasised two layers of identification that obscure the inner observer. This is an important observation. (1975, p. 121) The first layer is our social roles. When I meditate, I often hear the voice of "the teacher." I work as a teacher and when in meditation I have new experiences a voice begins as if it was standing in front of a group of students. I must release this voice before I can proceed. This is a subpersonality. The inner child and the inner critic are not the self. The next layer we go through is the inner commentator. This is our own inner voice, the one we associate with ourselves. Because we identify with the inner commentator this voice is difficult to release. Assagioli writes: "the last and perhaps most obstinate identification is with that which we consider to be our inner person, that which persists more or less during all the various roles we play" (1975, p. 121). In some versions of the Egg Diagram you often see a pair of glasses close to the observer to indicate this commentator. For the observer to appear as a clear, still and stable centre, this voice must quiet down.

Beginners do not often reach this place of silence, but can still be disidentified. There are different levels of disidentification. Here I will describe modes belonging to the personal self. The three levels I work with are:

Disidentification with strong attachment. You achieved a mental distance from the emotional state, but are not yet master of it, and perhaps even still under its control. The observer observes and prepares to break free. Disidentification can trigger a crisis, releasing identifications with a dominant role. Who are you, if you no longer need to be the self-effacing girl? Disidentification can leave an inner vacuum, a sense of emptiness until we find a new authentic centre for our identity. We can be disidentified and yet influenced by strong emotions.

Disidentification with moderate attachment. This is the most common form of observation. We are aware that we are affected by a psychological state. We cannot let go of it, although we are aware of its presence, but it cannot stop us from acting authentically. Here the personality is reasonably calm. We experience serenity and presence while thoughts, moods and sensations come and go. Our awareness is clear; we are connected to our self. We note fleeting inner and external impressions, while open to a self-awareness without content.

Disidentification without attachment. When we completely let go of everything in our consciousness, and the will is focused on presence and awareness, everything becomes quiet. The surface of consciousness is "free from ripples"; there is only the now, a sense of quiet and clear being. The sense of "I-amness" is strong but completely open. Strength (will) comes from the self's intention to discover and experience itself. There is an open self-awareness that clings to nothing other than the experience of pure self-awareness. There is a sense of being free – free to choose and be an authentic self.

DISIDENTIFICATION TECHNIQUES

A number of techniques are useful when working with disidentification.

Disidentification Exercise. I often practice disidentification and self-identification with the client. They usually record the exercise on their phones in order to have it available. I ask them to practice this exercise as often as possible, at least once a day, usually for about 10-15 minutes. An awareness meditation in the appendix provides an example.

Mirroring the client's loving witness. In the first session, I instruct my clients that I will train them in the ability to become a loving observer to their states of consciousness. I point out the distinction between them as observer and the states or material that emerges during therapy. I help them become conscious of identifications, emotional states or roles, (unless allowing the identification seems appropriate i.e. they need catharsis). When the client says, "I'm so angry with my mother," I say, "There's a side of you that is angry with your mother; you are the loving observer. Who is it in you that is angry? Can you embrace and accept the angry side?" This helps clients to adopt the attitude of disidentifying with the emotional state and identifying with the loving witness. There is more on this practice in the next chapter.

Externalisation of the content of consciousness: When the client is bound to a particular role with a strong attachment, for example, the victim, it may help to externalise this. This can be done several ways:

Chair work. We place a chair, representing the victim subpersonality, in front of the client. The clients' chair represents the loving witness. The client then moves chairs and from this position identifies with the victim and then in the next position, identify with the loving witness disidentifying from the victim.

Working with the hands. The client puts both hands on her thighs, palms up. Now ask her to place the victim in one hand and a subpersonality that resents being a victim in the other. In the middle is the client as a lovingly witness, moving between the poles. A psychotherapist trained in disidentification can facilitate this process.

Free drawing. Let the client draw her emotional states on a piece of paper. The emotion becomes an object externalized on the paper; the colours and shapes can be analysed and "felt" by the loving witness.

With the above presentation, I hope it becomes clear why Assagioli emphasized disidentification as the central tool in Psychosynthesis. Disidentification leads to self-identification. We cannot practice Psychosynthesis Psychotherapy if we do not master this technique. Disidentification is the first step on the road to the freedom *to be an authentic self*. The next step is the ability to be present, to contact the power of the will-to-be-a self, and then set a goal for the personal or transpersonal psychosynthesis.

We will examine these steps in the coming chapters, focussing on the self and Awareness Based Psychotherapy, and the will and Will Based psychotherapy.

Roberto Assagioli, 1888-1974

CHAPTER V

THE SELF
– THE WAY TO GREATER PRESENCE

"Because a good personal psychosynthesis is all that we
can look for in many of our patients the idea which is of
capital importance, and around which the entire personal
psychosynthesis revolves, is that of a personal self, of a
point of consciousness and self-awareness, coupled with
its realization and the use of its directing will"
(Assagioli, 1975, p. 87)

When Maja first started psychotherapy, it was obvious that she was identified with her mind. Her rationalisations often annoyed me and I could sense she was barely aware of her body and feelings. Her world consisted of sensible concepts, emotionally shallow and bodiless. She came to me because she was unhappy with her love life. She was 33 years old and had not yet started a family. Her last relationship ended five years ago; as her friends began to settle down and have children she felt increasingly desperate. She was involved with a married man, but knew he would never leave his wife, so this relationship caused her more pain than happiness.

I knew that our journey had to be a "descent" into the body and emotions. Presence and intimacy was our first task. When she spoke of her unhappiness there was no emotional "charge" in the room, and when she talked about the love she felt for the man she was seeing, I could not "feel" her.

We had to make her aware and present in her body. I suggested that she try to identify with the observer, and sense her physical and emotional responses to words like: "I am unhappy", "I love him." A greater depth to her experience would help her to become aware of a larger part of her inner world. My intention was to help her become a centre of pure self-awareness and will, a loving witness to her psychological processes.

In Chapter I we defined the self's consciousness as presence – the ability to be free, awake and aware in the present moment. We can see this as a loving presence that compassionately contains, observes and interacts with the content of the field of consciousness. In Chapter VI we will explore how the self is also a will – the will-to-be-self. Here we focus on presence as focused self-awareness. Awareness was important for Assagioli. "I speak much of awareness," he wrote. "Awareness is just this- to be aware all the time is not "pure awareness" or something transcendent. There is that of course. But the first awareness is to be aware of the interplay of the factors of the personality." (Undated 2)

The Observer

Presence constitutes the soul of Psychosynthesis. Its practitioners need to understand how to be present and how to work with presence with their clients. The personal self is Assagioli's second core concept and it is clear why he believed his understanding of it was unique to Psychosynthesis. It is precisely the definition of a central identity as pure self-awareness and will that sets Psychosynthesis apart from other psychotherapeutic approaches. This self is something quite different from the contents of consciousness, our thoughts, feelings and sensations. Assagioli was deeply inspired by the East's understanding of the self – especially the Yogic philosophy – and wrote extensively about it.

Pure consciousness, awareness and presence all point to the fundamental fact that we are conscious beings who can observe the content and flow of consciousness. Fundamentally we *are* consciousness. We see this in meditation when we "observe the observer." When we turn our consciousness towards its source, we find nothing but consciousness (and will, but more on this later).

We can observe the psychological processes taking place within us. The value of this is evident in a psychotherapeutic context. When working with clients, I use the metaphor of "the inner house," referring to the three levels of the Egg Diagram (see diagram: chapter two). The Lower Unconscious is the basement, the Middle Unconscious is the first floor, and the Superconscious is the second floor. Each level contains different energies and needs which affect the self (the observer). Some rooms even have subpersonalities that colour the atmosphere of the entire house.

It was clear that Maja mainly occupied the first floor of her inner house, whose rules are guided by rationality and logic. She was unaware of the resources stored at the lower and higher levels. Turning the light of consciousness inward, we illuminate what is hidden, and can see what affects our behaviour. This is easier said than done. Repressed, painful memories occupy these dark rooms. Yet doing so is an unavoidable prerequisite for freedom. We are in fact often enslaved to the reactions of the Lower Unconscious; becoming aware of them releases us.

Awareness Based Psychotherapy helps clients to be aware of the effect a particular subject has on their bodies, emotions and mind. In my practise, I first introduce clients to the idea of the inner house and the observer. Then I ask them to turn their attention to this inner world and what I refer to as the loving witness.

The client sits with eyes closed or open. I slowly guide their awareness to a quiet and attentive observation of their breath, body sensations, feelings and thoughts, relating to whatever subject we are working with. We can call this a reflective meditation on the content of the client's consciousness, an exercise in finding the right words for the energies that are sensed and observed. The exercise produces a sense of "coming home". We learn how to occupy all the floors of our inner house, creating a new and better atmosphere "at home."

When Maja spoke about her sadness, I asked where in her body she could feel it? Was it hot, cold, heavy, cutting, pulling? Looking at these emotional nuances, she realised that she was also angry, at herself and "the man". She felt used and that she had allowed herself to be used. We could say that Maja was emotionally and bodily illiterate. Her experience was limited to a small, rational part of her inner reality. Because of this she had a meagre vocabulary to describe what was happening in her inner world. But as the sessions progressed, she gained a greater intimacy with herself and her inner world.

"To come home to yourself" is to be with what is, without wanting to fix it or run away from it. This is the first step, but there is a second. We must not only witness our experiences, we must master them. We cannot be at home with ourselves while we are slaves to outgrown behavioural patterns. We must become "masters in our own house." That is the aim of Psychosynthesis.

Mastery requires love and will. As Assagioli points out these are essential:

"At the heart of the self there is both an active and a passive element, an agent and a spectator. Self-consciousness involves our being a witness – a pure, objective, loving witness – to what is happening within and without. In this sense the self is not a dynamic in itself but is a point of witness, a spectator, an observer who watches the flow. But there is another part of the inner self – the will-er or the directing agent – that actively intervenes to orchestrate the various functions and energies of the personality, to make commitments and to instigate action in the external world. So, at the centre of the self there is a unity of masculine and feminine, will and love, action and observation." (Keen, 1974)

LOVE IS NECESSARY

The foundation of Awareness Based Psychotherapy is *"to be with what is"*. At the first stage we observe the process. Next we contain, accept and include what we observe. Many of the subpersonalities squatting in our inner house are homeless, rejected and excluded. We must learn to love them. My method is:

Observe what is…
Love, what is…
Breathe through it…
Let it go…

Let's look at the role of love… Empathy is the key word here. To empathize with and understand the conditions from the inside is what unites and heals. Love is magnetic. It integrates and creates an intimacy – a unity- between the lover (self) and the beloved (the object).

The client may identify with that which repels or rejects the unwanted energies and subpersonalities. The therapist then must hold the space of acceptance. The ability to identify with the loving witness, will slowly ease the tension between what rejects and what is rejected. The loving witness can embrace both subpersonalities lovingly and achieve cooperation between the warring factors.

Maja needed to discover, contain and own her feelings. She could then recognise and relate to them. Initially I provided the containing and empathic centre, but by strengthening her identification with the loving witness, Awareness Based Psychotherapy soon passes this responsibility on to the client. Awareness Based Psychotherapy guides the client to an open, aware acceptance of life by revealing the truth that existentially speaking she *is* the loving witness. Through this process we gradually develop a centre of consciousness and will, one of the key elements of Psychosynthesis.

Will, because the client *will* to be a loving witness.

With its emphasis on the client *as self-awareness,* Psychosynthesis differs from other Awareness Based approaches such as Gestalt therapy. Our presence is a living being, a centre of pure self-awareness, not an *analytical* presence, neither an impersonal field. We affirm a centre, an inner identity, behind our thoughts, feelings and sensations. We call this the self. It is a *living being* whose fundamental feature is self-awareness and will. Psychosynthesis concerns the integration, harmonization and synthesis of the three levels of unconsciousness with the observer in the centre. This centre is necessary for integrating the conflicting parts of ourselves.

The observer is not an idea or theory; it is a fact of which we can become conscious. We may begin with the observer as an idea – most clients understand that they can observe the content of their consciousness. However, understanding is not the same as the awakening to the fact that one *is* consciousness, a pure consciousness, independent of thoughts feelings and sensations. This amounts to a revelation for the client. They have found the eye of the hurricane, a perpetually calm and stable point. The simplicity of their discovery astonishes them. It induces a sense of freedom; they can step back and observe powerful inner forces at work. Gradually they can be *present* with the depths (Lower Unconscious), the heights (the Superconscious) and the outer periphery of their being (the Collective Unconscious).

A strong identification with the mind makes our observations distant, cold and neutral. Including the body and emotion they become more intimate and immediate. This is because consciousness works *through* all three basic functions: thought, feeling and sensation. When we include intuition, we experience a beingness of light and connectedness.

Maja gradually became more present with her experiences. Her language became more nuanced. She could step out of the stream of consciousness and observe, could hold, breathe and chose how to respond. By disidentifying with her thoughts and identifying with the loving witness she gradually develop the loving observer.

FREEDOM THROUGH DISIDENTIFICATION

We've mentioned how essential it is for clients to practice disidentification. An important part of this process is the psychotherapist's ability to take the identity as an observer. If we observe the client closely, we can detect her identifications. When we act as observer, it becomes possible to see when the client identifies with a thought such as "I am angry, frustrated, ugly, stupid." We can then help the client to disidentify.

Sometimes the client is simply not able to disidentify. The pain could be too much, or what they gain from the identification is too important to give up. This is often the case when they identify with a "victim" subpersonality. The psychotherapist then holds the possibilities and gradually leads the client to meet these with an open heart. Repeated experiences of the freedom to choose how to respond to a situation or state, creates the need for more freedom. Transforming from a "victim" to a loving witness embracing the victim, is like moving from a closet to a spacious apartment. The victim may still be there, but is no longer "in our face" giving us more space to work with.

An Awareness Based approach works with the first, second and third person perspective simultaneously. A first-person perspective is fully identified with an emotional state. We deliberately experience being in full contact with all modes or aspects of our psychological states. If sufficiently anchored in her identify as the observer, the client can reflect on the experience while it happens. In a second person perspective we dialogue with the subpersonality or emotion, asking questions and listening to answers. The aim is to achieve cooperation, a loving exchange between the observer and the observed. In the third-person perspective there is greater distance. The client describes and talks about the subpersonality or emotion.

When we can master the flow and exchange of perspectives, we have a valuable tool for understanding and integration.

THE DEVELOPMENT OF PRESENCE – ITS DEPTH, HEIGHT AND WIDENESS

Presence and the loving witness is not something that develops spontaneously. It is a centre we must create internally before it becomes stable. Inner forces can trap us into certain psychological conditions. When we forget that we *are* consciousness, we limit ourselves to various roles or subpersonalities.

An observer has the potential to be both transcendent (when the observer is detached from what is observed) and immanent (when he is in a living and loving relationship with the observed). Transcendence observes something from above, from a distance; immanence gets inside it through empathic identification.

Being a transcendent observer implies a certain disidentification, yet we can still be affected by the experience. As mentioned, disidentification has different levels. Transcendence does not mean lofty spiritual experiences, a connotation often associated with the word. The observer can transcend emotions from the Lower Unconscious such as anger, jealousy or envy.

It is the same with immanence. The observer also has the potential to make a deep but conscious connection with our psychological or spiritual experiences. It is the nature of the observer to be something *other* than the content of consciousness.

We must emphasize that transcendence and immanence are *potentials*. In order to realise these potentials the observer's presence (depth, height, and breadth) must be developed. How present the self can be with the content of the Egg Diagram depends on the development of the self-line. The self and the development of presence form an individual line of development related to the psychological functions described in Chapter III.

The observer's relation to the Lower Unconscious is initially neither transcendent nor immanent to the states *below* it in the depths. Barriers of past conditioning, pain and fear must first be weakened with love and made conscious before they open to the observer. When this happens, the observer can express Lower Unconscious energies – sexual or aggressive – freely and spontaneously.

So too with the "heights" of the Superconscious. The observer cannot be present, observe and be in relation to the energies of the Superconscious unless the inner worlds of love and light are also conquered. This is what Self-Realization means: to expand and deepen relations between the self and the soul through the Bridge of Consciousness connecting the two.

The ability to be present in its wideness with political, social and cultural developments depends on the empathy (immanence) and span of the self's consciousness (transcendence). Breadth of perspective also includes our ability to identify psychological and spiritual influences coming from the Collective Unconscious from the biological to the spiritual levels.

We must emphasize that presence, the observer's focused self-awareness develops in tandem with our other psychological functions. We use our mind to know, our emotions to empathise and our body to act.

Awareness Based Psychotherapy strengthens a client's ability to be present (awake, containing, breathing, letting go) with what *is* at any given time. It must, however, become a daily practice, something Assagioli recommended for disidentification.

To develop presence we must practice meditation. According to Assagioli, meditation is "the central technique which helps amplify effectively all the other techniques" (Freund, 1983). And that: "In order to strengthen and make stable the pure self-awareness of the observer, it is necessary to have periods of inner silence, gradually longer, to make what is called the void in the field of consciousness. Then one discovers another important function of the self: that it is not merely an observer, but it can also be active in modifying the personality. That is, it can direct and regulate the various functions of the psyche. It can be a *will-er*." (Assagioli in Besmer, 1974)

Speaking with Sam Keen (1974), Assagioli confirmed that the disidentification technique resembles Vipassana meditation (Buddhist insight meditation). "The goal of these exercises is to learn to disidentify at any time of the day, to dis-associate the self from any overpowering emotion, person, thought or role and assume the vantage point of the detached observer". Such practice reveals the self as a centre of pure self-awareness and will.

Awareness meditation is essential to Psychosynthesis and we can practice self centring throughout daily life. The aim is not a peak experience, but a gradually strengthening of presence. Therapists must also practice presence when working with clients. Presence allows us to observe what is happening inside ourselves and in the client's field. We must encourage our clients to practice it from the very start of the therapy. Working with Maja I encouraged her continually to observe and notice her reactions when she talked about her processes.

Through the observer we can harmonize and synthesize our inner conflicts. It is the fulcrum around which we observe, love and master our different energies. As Assagioli states: "Therefore, Psychosynthesis, first, second and third, is the working from the centre". (Undated 2)

We can cover some ground without meditation if the intellect is used as a neutral and objective analytical function. Assagioli refers to the "inner person" in the last chapter, and I suggest it is our identification with the intellect and commentator. When the self identifies with the intellect, it becomes the centre. Because we are often driven by irrational unconscious beliefs that the intellect has unconsciously adopted, this centre's freedom is limited. Often we can go no further because the client, the psychotherapist or both are not motivated to develop the real centre. Developing presence is like learning to play the violin. Once we discover the observer and its dynamic will-to-be-self, we can play all the strings of the personality, and our life becomes music.

THE INTEGRATION OF THE PERSONALITY

Personal psychosynthesis aims to unite the forces of the personality around the self, hence the importance of integration. In Chapter III we defined a self-actualized personality as someone who can freely assert his or her uniqueness. When the disparate aspects of their personality are integrated, they become focused, independent, authentic, definite, and strong.

There are, however, types of integration when the observer is not the centre. Identifying with presence and self-awareness occurs at an advanced stage of development. Usually, one or more roles connected to a psychological function constitute the centre around which our lives are organized.

For example, a woman identified with her role as mother (based primarily on the feeling function) organizes her life around children and the family. Here she is authoritative, persevering and independent. Naturally, this is a very limited identity; many inner resources may not be activated and actualized. There is nothing wrong with this. From her perspective it is an authentic life choice. But it has consequences. She may face a crisis when the children leave home, or, if she is uneducated or unemployed, she may become dependent on her husband or social services.

Other forms of integration involve one-sided and dominant roles such as one's career, sports or social life. We may be strong, integrated and focused in these roles, but behind the scenes, we can experience great inner conflicts. Parts of our nature have been repressed and excluded from our identity, leaving an unbalanced personality. An artist may have an inferiority complex because he is uneducated. A successful CEO may have a string of failed relationship behind her.

With Maja, she unconsciously shifted among three sides of her nature, which constituted her centre. I illustrate her situation using the Egg Diagram used by Assagioli (1983c). A pair of glasses near the self symbolizes the "inner commentator" is inserted by me. As mentioned, Assagioli described three different self-identifications: Subpersonalities or "Personages", the commentator or "Person" and pure self-awareness (see 1975, p. 121). Here three dominant roles (subpersonalities) oc-

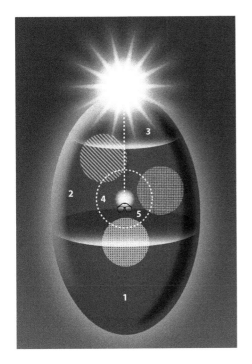

Maja's three dominating subpersonalities

cupy most of the field of consciousness and the centre; they constitute Maja's identity.

Maja came to me because her self-image as a woman suffered and she yearned for a warm and nurturing relationship. This role inhabits the lower circle and its needs relate to the love needs in Maslow's Hierarchy of Needs.

The middle circle represents her professional identity as IT manager in a large media agency. Maja was happy with her work. She was good at her job and was recognised for this. This role made her self-reliant and financially independent, and she saw her job as the most stable aspect of her life.

The upper circle represents her "inner philosopher" and her interest in life's big questions. She was curious about the meaning of life and death. She had read some self-development literature, but also ancient Greek philosophy. That the upper circle reaches into the Superconscious illustrates that abstract and reflective thought can connect with "something greater". Maja thrived within the mental world, but it was her identification with her intellect that caused the problems in her love life.

When she started therapy Maja was not aware of the self as the observer/presence, and her will was tied to her work identity. The three circles in the oval diagram show only their centre of gravity relative to the primary motivation of the subpersonality. Depending on the psychological state of each subpersonality, they may go up or down the Egg Diagram. In reality things are more nuanced than what a diagram can illustrate; in Chapter VIII we will explore subpersonalities further.[11]

We become much more free from our different roles when the observer is the integrating centre of the personality. We can move in and out of roles and subpersonalities easier then. We relate to life with a sense of playfulness because we *know* that our identity does not depend on the roles we play. This freedom re-

---

11 Assagioli, 1983c, gives many examples of these scenarios.

quires constant struggle. We must fight many battles before we liberate ourselves from strong identifications with certain roles. Whatever the loss in our love life, career or social status, they offer opportunities to develop trust in the will and to recognise that we need not identify too strongly with anything in the external world. This inner detachment creates greater flexibility. We can take more risks because we can handle the danger of reaching out for something new. We become more creative, courageous and committed; in other words, a self-actualized personality.

The observer does not emerge spontaneously out of the blue, it must be won through our struggles in life. An extrovert can be introspective and practice inner observation and know nothing about disidentification. Life will itself teach him to disidentify. To be conscious of our inner observer is an advantage, but not necessary. The observer is an existential fact that one way or another we awaken to, but clearly a determined development of the observer saves many unnecessary struggles. That meditation and yoga are popular suggests that the experience of the self as pure self-awareness is spreading.

Ideally the integration of the personality is guided by the self as a loving dynamic observer. This, as mentioned, is our personal psychosynthesis. Humanistic or altruistic values do not necessarily motivate us at this stage; we may just want to get the most out of our lives and relationships.

THE PSYCHOTHERAPIST AS THE EXTERNAL UNIFYING CENTRE

Developing self-awareness alone is a great challenge. Presence and the will are subtle and are obscured by our identifications with ideas, feelings and external things. Here the living contact with another self-aware person is crucial. This may happen in therapy, or a meditation teacher or good friend can help. But when working to release ties to the past, things are different. This requires professional help, a psychotherapist trained to work with repressions, resistance and transferences.

Assagioli sees the therapist as: "not only pointing out and suggesting to the patient, as Jung does, the goal of his "individuation", but encouraging and educating him from the outset to practice active methods of acquiring an increasingly clear self-consciousness, the development of a strong will and the mastery and right use of his impulsive emotional, imaginative and mental energies, and to avail himself of all means of gaining independence of the therapist." (1967b)

We must clarify this with our clients. Assagioli mentions first the development of self-consciousness, then the will. As Psychosynthesis focuses on the role of the centre this makes sense. It concerns the client's ability to be a loving witness capable of independent choices (the will) and implementing them in life. The self develops via the mirroring or feedback between the psychotherapist and the client.

When we psychotherapists develop our inner observer we are able to recognise our client's observer and help him to become his own loving witness. We can help our clients to *disidentify from limiting self-perceptions* such as "no one loves me", "I'm so angry," and "I am not attractive." This shows our clients the *freedom* that disidentification offers. As the psychotherapist nurtures a relationship in which the client takes responsibility for his own life, the client's autonomy and the will-to-be-self is also strengthened.

In short, the psychotherapist aims to be an authentic mirror for the client's own self-awareness, and in a broader sense, for the link between her self and soul. For Assagioli the therapist "must, to some extent, take on the role and task as protector, counsellor and guide. In dream symbolism, says Jung, he frequently appears under the aspect of the "wise old man" and corresponds to what the Indians calls "guru". (1967b) Here the psychotherapist acts as both healer and teacher.

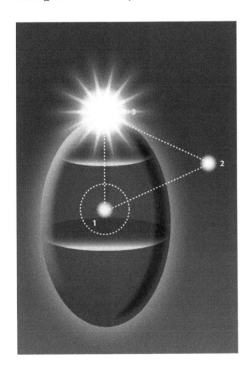

The therapist as External Unifying Centre

Assagioli illustrates this relationship in the diagram below, where he also describes four different client therapist relationships (1967b).

The star outside the individual psyche (2) represents the therapist. The therapist acts as a link or bridge between the individual self (1) and soul (3). When the client is not in direct "vertical" contact with the soul, the therapist can help establish this. The therapist becomes a "role model", or "catalyst" for the development. The therapist acts as an external unifying centre helping the client to find his own centre. The star on the border of the Superconscious indicates that the therapist holds a transpersonal perspective and ideally expresses this to clients.

Working with Maja I focused on developing her feminine side and feeling function. In strengthening her feminine self-esteem as a woman, my gender played a role. Maja needed to be seen by a man who could understand and contain her despair about her love life.

The Awareness Based approach helped her to observe more of her personality than her mind, with which she was identified. She recognised that her identity as the loving witness strengthened her relationship to her body and emotional needs. Disidentifying from the body did not prevent her from being grounded in it, the opposite was the result due to her warm appreciation of it. As a result of this work she decided to leave the married man. She accepted that she had to stand up for herself and her dignity as a woman. She needed a man to be fully committed to her, and this meant choosing herself first. The will-to-be-self gave her the strength to stand alone and the freedom to find the right man.

THE RELATIONSHIP BETWEEN THE SELF AND THE SOUL

Chapter X concerns the relationship between the self and the soul, but I will briefly touch on it here. There is one self – Assagioli was very clear on this – but it unfolds at different levels. The consciousness, inner light, and presence is the same. The degree of awareness differs; what the self can consciously contain and include determines its "size." An enlightened person will know with certainty and from experience that her pure consciousness is also my consciousness. The difference between us is the individual intention and purpose (the will) we have regarding our evolutionary role in the whole, the universal Self.

The difference between the personal and the Transpersonal Self depends on how free the observer is; how transcendent and immanent we are in relation to the content of consciousness on all levels. When we experience the *personal self* as pure self-awareness, a sense of separateness remains. There is a distinct feeling of an "I" that is quite different from "you". Here the observer is still limited to the mental field, which creates this duality.

When we pass into the Superconscious, awareness expands beyond our physical limits into infinity. Thought stops; we lose our mental chains and find ourselves completely free and peaceful, as if a straightjacket had been removed. We can still think, but it's like squeezing infinity into a box. There is still a "me" (I-am-ness), and full identity. But it is a me that is liberated.

In Awareness Based Psychotherapy we don't often have the opportunity to work with the spiritual experience of self. But it can happen if the Psychosynthesis Psychotherapist practices awareness meditation seriously. A powerful exercise is to maintain eye contact with the client and just be, immersing oneself in the consciousness of the other.

Deep eye contact can instil peace and freedom, if the therapist knows how to communicate these states. I have practiced this for years and occasionally a client spontaneously recognises the value of "just being." Once we sat for 45 minutes in silence. We knew that something transpersonal, a deeper being, was activated. Time stops, two souls are together in an endless now, a profound peace. Afterwards the client said: "This is the first time ever that someone else has been able to be with me in my deepest being."

In the next chapter we will discuss the will and see how we can strengthen our own and our clients' freedom to- be- self.

CHAPTER VI

THE WILL
– THE WAY TO POWER

*"The will is the central power of our individuality, the
innermost essence of our self; therefore, in a certain sense, the
discovery of the will means the discovery of our true being"*
(Assagioli, Undated 12)

Assagioli's third core concept is the will: "The aspects of the fully developed human will are the strong will, the skilful will, the good will, and the Transpersonal Will.". (1974, p. 15) The will is associated with our essential identity. We know that the self not only observes but also *directs*. Assagioli considered this aspect of the self the cornerstone of Psychosynthesis. If the self is only an observing, loving witness, it can do nothing but passively observe while powerful inner forces or people try to dominate or control us. With the discovery of the will we see that we can take control over our lives. With the right use of the will we can master inner and outer psychological influences. Through the will, we recognise the power of authenticity and the freedom to *express* ourselves. There is no greater power than being ourselves.

Assagioli describes it in the following way: "The man of weak will is like a cork on the ocean, tossed by every wave; or like the weather vane, turned about by every gust of wind. He is the slave not only of the will of others and all external circumstances, but also of his drives and desires. He is unable to make adequate use of his talents and aptitudes; he is unable to live up to his convictions." (Undated 12)

Assagioli emphasizes the fact that we don't *have* a will, we *are* a will. That is: "The will is the central power of our individuality, the innermost essence of our self; therefore, in a certain sense, the discovery of the will means the discovery of our true being." (Assagioli, Undated 12) The will is something we *experience*; as such it is difficult to explain in theory. As with beauty, the will is subjective. Can we explain to someone the beauty of a sunset if they have not had intimate contact with nature? The will is an inner, dynamic living force; fundamentally it is the will-to-be-who-I am.

I would like to share a personal experience to illustrate this:

"I'd been meditating for 5 hours, only interrupted by a 10-minute interval. My focus was on observing the content of my consciousness. Nothing specific was supposed to happen, except from me being present in the moment. During the first few hours my mind was filled with a cacophony of impressions, but now a sense of clarity emerged and the many impressions no longer disturbed me. Sitting with this clarity any thoughts, moods and sensations faded into the background, and it became obvious that only consciousness is real. I am consciousness; an awake and aware space of quiet existence. Then the question arose: "What would I be without the content of consciousness?" "Nothing" was the prompt reply. I recognized the answer yet ... who was asking? Who was choosing to meditate? Who was maintaining the intention to sit and just observe? Who chose to stop the meditation? Who allowed these questions to arise? This reflection made it clear to me that as long as I am in a body and have to function in a manifest universe, I must act. Not to act is also an act. *Choosing* not to act is an act. There is a will inside us that always wants something and it becomes active as soon as I act. This means choosing presence, a thought, a feeling, a physical act. What is this force? Who is it? ... This question was too interesting not to pursue, so the focus of my meditation shifted character, something in me made this choice, and my journey changed."

Consciousness is fundamentally without boundaries and universal. We can therefore call the self as the loving witness the *open self*.

Consciousness is a universal backdrop of awareness – a ground of being – and by being in the present moment we can observe the content of consciousness. The will is a dynamic *force* that expresses itself through individuality and gives our consciousness focus and direction. Essentially, we are consciousness with a purpose, which ultimately is the will-to-be-a self. In other words, we all have a living dynamic force inside us impelling us towards the realization of the self. And the will, the dynamic face of the self, accomplishes this through purpose, intention, choice and direction. The will expresses the universal in us as individuality and in that sense we can say that through the conscious application of our will we become the *unique self*. The experience of pure will can best be described as purpose. In contrast to the open self, the will centralises the energies around a point/centre. In terms of energy we can say that our true identity is both an energy field (openness) and a particle (a point) in space. This is – admittedly – a very subtle description which can only be understood through direct experience.

Assagioli gives the following description: "When we experience ourselves as "selves," as subjects, we frequently have an experience that can be summed up

in this sentence: "I am a force, a cause." This is an experience of the human will."
(Miller, 1972)

The will can be experienced at different levels. Implicit in this perspective is the existence of one universal consciousness (God, Brahman, the One), which seeks to unfold its universality through individuality. This means that every person, every being, every creation, is potentially a unique expression – or emanation – of an underlying unity. In Christianity this equates to the notion of God incarnating in Jesus Christ. We all have a "Christ" or "Buddha" nature, but that does not mean we should copy Buddha or Christ. We must realize our own unique divine nature through the will-to-be-self. When we experience this aspect of the will, we recognise the soul's Transpersonal Will. Yet the will knocks on the door of our personality well in advance of any sign of spiritual inclinations.

THE DISCOVERY OF THE WILL

We first notice the presence of the will as a call from our unique self when we awaken to the need to become a self. This call for freedom and independence is often connected to a crisis. The will is the longing for freedom and authenticity that emerge as we attempt to liberate ourselves from various dependencies and identifications. Assagioli describes it thus: "one keynote of the will is freedom – freedom to choose and to act the way we want to." (Miller, 1972)

The pain we experience when we are unable to be ourselves acts as a stimulant to the will. We may need outside confirmation of our identity. It then rests on shaky ground and it becomes difficult for us to establish appropriate boundaries. Or we may be dominated by inner inclinations that run counter to our self-image. In either case, we are not masters in our house. We are tossed to and fro by habits and desires, which diminish our self-respect. These dependencies pose great limitations to our lives.

As these examples show, will and desire are not the same. You may have a *will* to do something, but you do something different. Will and desire are both powerful, but the will is *always* connected to identity; the will to be a unique self in action. Desire is often about something outside ourselves, something we *want*, affirmation, security, power or something we want to avoid. Yet we may also want to be ourselves, which is an important desire that can lead to the will.

The will is deeply connected to boundaries. It is through our boundaries that we define our individuality and uniqueness. Paradoxically we free ourselves through our boundaries, because only when we define our identity through our conscious choices, we become unique. When we stop imitating others and focus on ourselves and our sense of being, we can choose our identity, and gradually liberate ourselves from non-authentic behavior.

Assagioli describes how the will can emerge as a response to the need to stand up for ourselves and the values and needs we identify with at any given time. We may call this "Identity strength", a force that provides us with a sense of grounding and integrity. Here the will is a way to greater power.

The will gives us the courage to end an unhappy relationship or leave an unfulfilling career. The strong will is often founded on a sense of dignity, the conviction that we are a valuable expression of something great and important – the soul. But we have to *choose* our self if we are to recognize ourselves in our actions. This often involves a crisis where we must, as it were, sacrifice our dependencies on the fire of freedom.

Our actual identity, the roles and self-perceptions we have at any given time, are a result of our unconscious and conscious choices. Self-images can represent our false self if they are unconscious imitations. But they can also represent our true selves if they are an expression of a conscious choice. The will enables us to disidentify but also to identify. The will says: "I am not this or that – but this". We *are* that which we *chose* to think, feel and act, even if our choices are based on social and cultural influences. Conscious or unconscious choices have the same effect- they create identity. Our choices always have consequences; making conscious choices allows us the freedom to choose something new.

Choosing new self-perceptions has consequences too. Attachments and emotions formed by previous choices revolt against the new will. Awakening to these polarities is painful, but it is the tension between past and present choices that can shape our future identity. When we decide to become who we are as unique individuals our personal psychosynthesis begins.

WILL BASED PSYCHOTHERAPY

Applying these insights into an Awareness- and Will Based Psychotherapy, the psychotherapist will need to especially focus on the client's identity. Awareness and will are essential to this. We need to get to know the client before we start working with his or her issues. Assagioli refers to this initial therapeutic stage as "Thorough knowledge of the client's personality".

Psychosynthesis is about helping the client to become an authentic personality, independent of where in the Egg Diagram their identity is located. Because our clients' issues can be worked with in several ways, we first need a thorough understanding of their self-perception, needs and values. Otherwise the client may adapt to the psychotherapy instead of the therapy to the client.

The first thing I ask the client is, "Where is your journey going? How do you want to grow in this process?" I use metaphors like "being a captain in your own life", seeing the client as setting a course and steering the way; another useful metaphor is to "be master in your own house." I emphasize that there is a force in our lives, the *will- to- be-self*. It is important to explore this "will to self"; it drives our need for authenticity, individuality and the freedom to be oneself.

When the client together with the psychotherapist defines her goals, her will becomes focused. The goal can be anything, from a wish to achieve greater presence or spontaneity to the courage to set boundaries. These goals may not normally be associated with the will because the will is not understood for what it is, the *intention* behind any conscious action. When we have a sufficiently focused will, an inner attraction develops, guiding our psychological energies in a specific direction.

Maja wanted her love life to function; she *willed* to succeed in love. Our first sessions were about her taking responsibility for this, which she did by defining what a good love relationship is. Next, she committed herself to action. We should never make decisions for our clients because it is by taking on this responsibility that they develop strength.

In Maja's case she needed to end her affair with the married man. The relationship was unworthy of her and not aligned with her needs and values, something she had long known. With him she did not feel important. She had not chosen herself and therefore did not demand anything from the love she shared in a relationship, something her affair with a married man symbolised. She knew she depended on the confirmation he gave her, and that the hope that he would one day be hers was an illusion. But she lacked the will power to act on this.

Her will and her desire were in conflict. Her will, connected her to freedom and dignity. It told her she deserved better. The will comes from the soul and as our self-awareness increases, it is reflected in the self. It is the evolutionary urge pushing us out of our comfort zones towards more freedom, love and greatness. The will expresses the force from the archetypal king and queen, the soul and the universal Self. Our individual interpretation of this force, the values and images we attach to this power, is an expression of where in the Egg Diagram we currently reside.

When we awaken to our will, our sense of direction becomes clear, whether at a personal or transpersonal level. Maja needed to confront the sense of worthlessness that kept her in a relationship in which she was not seen or chosen because of who she is. During therapy she realized this reflected her lack of self-worth. She now chose to focus her will on developing her identity and self-worth as a woman because this represented her greatest limitation.

According to Assagioli, when we work to strengthen a client's will the therapist can take on a "father therapy" style:

"The therapist, you see, has two major roles: *the motherly role and the fatherly role*. The motherly role of the therapist is in order in the first part of the treatment, especially in the more serious cases. It consists in giving a sense of protection, understanding, sympathy and encouragement. What a wise mother does. It is a direct *helping* by the therapist of the client.

The fatherly role, on the other hand, can be summed up as the *training to independence*. The true fatherly role, as I see it, is to encourage, to arouse the inner energies of the child and to show him the way to independence. Therefore, the fatherly function is to awaken the will of the client." (Miller, 1972)

The will regulates all the other psychological functions. This ensures the integrity of our personal and spiritual development, and will eventually liberate our personality. To make this happen we must teach our clients to use the *active techniques* that can help them to master psychological energies. We all experience fear, resistance, rebellion or paralysis when we need to develop new sides of ourselves.

Assagioli was inspired by Eastern yoga techniques, especially Raja Yoga and its eightfold path to liberation. It is in this light that the application of these techniques should be seen, especially disidentification, visualization and the will.

According to Assagioli the "principal aims and tasks" of psychotherapy are:

1. "The elimination of the conflicts and obstacles, conscious and unconscious that block this development.

2. The use of active techniques to stimulate the psychic functions that are still weak and immature. (1967a)

There are also "a large number of active techniques designed to:

1. Awaken latent energies, particularly in the higher unconscious.

2. Develop the constitutionally weak functions and those arrested at an infantile stage.

3. Transmute the overabundant bio-psychic energies and those that cannot be discharged or expressed in direct ways.

4. Discipline and regulate (without repressing or removing) the manifestation of all psychic energies of every level, promoting their constructive and efficient utilisation and creative expression.

5. Harmonise the various functions and energies, thereby constructing an integrated human personality.

6. Promote the introduction of the individual into society by means of harmonious interpersonal and group relations". (1967a)

The will leads us to freedom, and is the antidote to dependency and victimhood. Father Therapy can therefore be seen as a "freedom project" which supports the client's self-actualization and Self-realization. If we leave out the will, we run the danger of the client regressing. This especially so if the psychotherapist focuses on caretaking and Mother Therapy, which perpetuates the client's dependency on the psychotherapist and is in direct contrast to the values of psychosynthesis. Assagioli said that the therapist should encourage and train the client "from the outset to practice active methods of acquiring an increasingly clear self-consciousness, the development of a strong will and the mastery and right use of his impulsive emotional, imaginative and mental energies, and to avail himself of all means of gaining independence of the therapist." (1967b)

In therapy it makes sense to start by strengthening awareness and will. After all they constitute the central aspects of our identity and steer the course of our lives. When the psychotherapist is mirroring the client's will, it is a good idea to name the client's chair the "director's chair", "captain's chair" or "instructor's chair". Here decisions are made. The intention is to help the client to consciously identify with the loving witness who is making decisions. Other aspects of the client can be objectified by other chairs representing her different subpersonalities. These can either be supportive or opposed to the client's goals.

Most mirroring occurs in the relational field between the client and psychotherapist. When the psychotherapist has authentic authority, both professionally and personally, this power is transmitted to the client. When the client realizes that the psychotherapist's intention is to liberate her so she can be what she chooses and has the potential to become, the client experiences being seen in her *strength*.

This does not mean that the therapist *unequivocally* supports all the client's beliefs. On the contrary, the Will Based Psychotherapist must challenge the client's assumptions. The strength of the client's convictions are tried and tested against the needs and values that have been identified in the therapeutic process. At some point in the psychosynthetic approach the psychotherapist openly explains its philosophy to the client. If the therapeutic objective is accepted, the psychotherapist takes on the roles of guide and healer in relation to this. The healer function is concerned with bringing love and understanding to the psychological processes (the mother role). And in our role as guides we train our clients to become a loving witness who with power can express their identities in action (the father role).

The transference of power is central to Awareness and Will Based Psychotherapy. It relies on the psychotherapist's ability to see the potentialities and possibilities in the client which have not yet come to bloom. The therapist's faith and certainty in the client's ability to become fully himself is essential to the psychotherapeutic relationship. It enables the client to see *himself* as the psychotherapist does and to *identify* with the therapeutic vision. In this sense, the psychotherapist becomes an external unifying centre reflecting the client's deepest values and needs.

It is important to have the *skilful will* in mind. If we understand life from an evolutionary perspective, we see that it is a journey towards more consciousness. We see that our sense of identity evolves as our values and needs change. We must choose our identity with care and hold it lightly in our awareness. Evolution demands that we do not identify with, or become too attached to anything. This perspective can be introduced in therapy using statements such as: "It is true in the present moment."

THE STRONG, GOOD AND SKILFUL WILL

Let us now briefly refine the description of the will. In *The Act of Will* Assagioli differentiates between three aspects as well as three levels of will. The three aspects are the strong, good and skilful will. The three levels are personal, transpersonal and universal will. Fundamentally there is only one will, the universal will, the evolutionary force behind the creation. But this will unfolds in various ways depending on the person's level of development. Here is how Assagioli distinguishes between the strong and good will:

"At the centre of the self there is a unity of masculine and feminine, will and love, action and observation" (Keen, 1974) The self contains the polarity between the masculine-feminine, which is universally applicable in the cosmos. In the East it is referred to as Yin-Yang or Shiva-Shakti. The will can thus be masculine or feminine:

"The will is not merely assertive, aggressive and controlling. There is the accepting will, the yielding will, the dedicated will. You might say that there is a feminine polarity to the will—the willing surrender, the joyful acceptance of the other functions of the personality." (Assagioli in Keen, 1974)

The Strong Will is the most basic and familiar expression of will; it is the masculine assertion of *identity*. It is the dynamic power and ego strength which enable the emergence of the self. The strong will can easily be abused; hence its somewhat bad reputation. But we must recognize that the strong will is essentially the will-to-be-self and is indispensable when we are working to become a free human being. If we are self-centred, the strong will can damage our relationships and cause trouble in other social contexts. It is not inherently evil, but it can only unfold according to the underlying values, wisdom or consciousness that controls it.

The strong will relates to the "fire-aspect" of the self and comes directly from spirit. This force insists on becoming all that it may be. The will's strength depends on how much purpose we invest in a goal i.e. how strong is the will to be oneself. Whether the strong will is destructive or constructive depends on its balance with the good will. When influenced by the loving polarity of the self, the will becomes the good will.

The Good Will: "It may be said to be an expression of love" (Assagioli, 1974, p. 90). The will is essentially about expressing our *identity in action*; for example, setting goals and achieving them. The good will is effective because it teaches us how to cooperate; it creates healthy, constructive relationships with others in order to realize common goals. People are often lacking in either the love or the will aspect of the self; they are loving and caring but lack strong will, or are strong and powerful but lack good will. We must balance and synthesize our love and will, which, Assagioli knew, is not an easy feat.

"It calls for persistent vigilance, for constant awareness from moment to moment... But this awareness, this attitude of maintaining a conscious inner "presence," does not stop with the observation of what "happens" within oneself and in the external world. It makes possible the *active intervention* and *commitment* on the part of the self, who is not only an observer, but also a *willer*, a directing agent of the play of the various functions and energies." (1974, p. 101) Here we return to the intention behind Awareness and Will Based Psychotherapy: helping our clients to become a loving witness who can master life using the strong, good and skilful will. The self's core is static, the consciousness open and powerful. When the self expresses itself in *action* it does so through the seven psychological functions.

Here the skilful will plays a major part.

The skilful will. The decision to express our self in a new and authentic way is exciting, yet it also brings fear, inertia, and other kinds of inner and outer resistance. When we decide to put the *will-to-be-ourselves* into practice, our approach can be unbalanced. If our will is too strong we may try to repress our conflicting emotions, which can result in a too rigid personality. If we emphasize the good will, we might not be able to will at all; we may be too tolerant of inner resistance and prefer to passively go with the flow.

We must then call on the skilful will. As Assagioli writes:

"The essential function of the skilful will, which we need to cultivate, is the ability to develop that strategy which is most effective and which entails the greatest economy of effort, rather than the strategy that is most direct and obvious." (1974, p. 47)

Strategy is the key idea here, as is "economy of effort". Much energy is wasted on conflicts created by the strong will or by the good will's lack of control.

Assagioli maintains that willpower is not based solely on the strength of the will. Rather he sees it as a function that can awaken, regulate and direct all the psychological functions and as such utilize the power inherent in our body, feelings, desires, ideas, thought and intuition.

In *The Act of Will*, Assagioli describes the psychological laws which activate these psychological forces. A few examples must suffice. The power of visualization is well known in meditation and mental training. It is based on the creative force of the imagination. Visualizing something can awaken and direct our psychological energies. If we visualize the sun as if it was located near our heart, emanating love to ourselves and the world, then we will gradually experience this love as a reality. Images are very powerful; a fact the advertising industry knows how to exploit.

Another aspect of the six stages of the skilful will, which I can only briefly mention, relates to how we realize an idea, from its conception to its execution. The stages are similar to the kind of "process thinking" we often find in coaching.

DEVELOPING MAJA'S STRONG, GOOD AND SKILFUL WILL

In my work with Maja my initial aim was to strengthen her *strong will* and her sense of identity as a woman. I did this by consistently acknowledging her will-to-be-self

and encouraging her inner exploration. How did she experience her will
to have a good love life? How did the
body feel, or her emotions, and what
pictures did she have of it?

We also worked with her skilful will.
I objectified her will to love with a
chair that represented the "dignified
woman". Her usual seat was the director's chair; it represented the self,
the caretaker of her inner crew (the
subpersonalities), the loving and
powerful witness. The other chair
represented the Ideal Model of her
inner woman (see diagram). During our sessions I often asked if she
could sit in the chair representing
her inner woman.

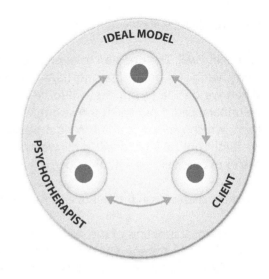

The Ideal model of the dignified woman

The role-playing and visualization awakened Maja's desire to express her femininity with self-worth. Sitting in the ideal woman's chair she could feel the values and
needs that were important to her love life. She explored what kind of man she was
attracted to. She also drew a picture of her inner woman, which she scanned and
used as screen saver on her PC.

We recorded a short heart centred meditation on her cell phone, where she visualized herself as a "worthy woman". The exercise produced an energy and a sense of
herself as a noble being. Our work together gave birth to a dignified and authentic
inner woman. With Maja as the loving and directing witness, the inner woman
gained greater power of self- expression. Eventually Maja was able to end the relationship with the married man.

In Will Based Psychotherapy the client is encouraged to *act* on her inner discoveries. We therefore planned scenarios where Maja had to set boundaries and be
direct about her needs, and then we discussed the result in our next session. In
some sessions she sat in different chairs and rehearsed imaginary conversations
with people. Through this she learned what it meant to be authentic in her deal-
ings with the world.

As mentioned, working to develop new personality traits and behavior will most
likely create inner resistance. Previously dominant habits resist change. Old be-

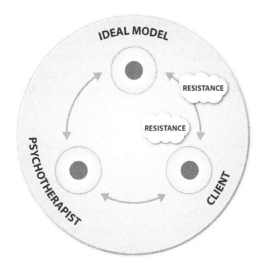

The Ideal Model creates inner resistance

liefs, self-images and insecurities will rebel. The skilful will is all important when working with these forces.

When Maja decided to act on her new insights, she was apprehensive, particularly so in the months leading up to the break up. We placed the chairs representing the obstacles before her Ideal Model and explored these inner voices (see diagram). It soon became clear that her "inner child" and "inner teenager" were producing this fear. Working with these subpersonalities is the main focus of Chapter VIII.

When the fear was too great Maja could not act. We worked with these obstacles according to the three perspectives described in the last chapter. We put her fearful teens in chairs, and she described each one while sitting in the observer's chair (3. person). She then changed chairs and dialogued with the other subpersonalities in the room (2. person). She identified deeply with each subpersonality; this gave her valuable insight into the actual fear (1. person). The inner resistance is represented by the fearful teenagers in the diagram above.

These exercises released repressed feelings (catharsis) and allowed Maja insights into the different layers of her personality. It illustrated the kind of work where, as Assagioli says, we: "transform the overabundant bio-psychic energies and those that cannot be discharged or expressed in a direct way." Her inner teenagers felt a deep longing for her absent father. Great shame accompanied this and could not be expressed in her unsatisfactory relationship. Her inner teenagers had learned to adapt and not be a "burden" in relation to men. This submissive and pleasing role is a classic example of a false self that has developed in response to not having one's authentic needs met.

We can see how Maja's will satisfies the needs of both the Ideal Model and the conflicting subpersonalities. Maja as the observer uses her will to activate the imagination, emotions, body and thoughts in order to redeem the accumulated energies. This enabled completely new sides of her personality to develop. As Assagioli told Sam Keen:

"But in the normal person the will can function to lessen or to eliminate the conflict by recognizing a hierarchy of needs and arranging for an appropriate satisfaction of all needs. The central will distributes the tasks to other parts of the personality. Let me use an analogy that is central to my thinking: The will is like the conductor of an orchestra. He is not self-assertive but is rather the humble servant of the composer and of the score. " (1974, Keen)

Maja and I worked directly with the inner world of the different subpersonalities. They feared the consequences of having an authentic female identity. Through guided meditations she explored her inner house and identified the various self-images she had throughout her life. Because Maja now knew how to be a loving witness, these meditations created more space for her subpersonalities. She gained insights into how she could engage with her "voices" and satisfy their needs through the loving energy from her heart. We can compare working with the skilful will with the psycho-spiritual techniques used in yoga. As our sessions progressed her will-to-be-self became stronger, more loving and intelligent. She also became more *assertive*. She experienced greater flow in her life and an effortless will to simply be herself, especially in her interactions with men.

The day she told me she had left the married man was momentous. She was not bitter about what had previously seemed a betrayal on his part. She could see how they both had "used" each other to meet certain needs, which they thought could not be otherwise met. She was now ready to look to the future and to embody her new Ideal Model. She felt freer to be herself and was determined to succeed in love.

In the chapter on the soul, we will go deeper into the Transpersonal Will's function and purpose, but now the time has come to deal with the Ideal Model.

CHAPTER VII

THE IDEAL MODEL
– THE WAY TO FOCUS

"Individual psychosynthesis can be said to consist essentially
in the actualization of one's own ideal model"
(Assagioli, 1974, p. 185)

Let's take a closer look at Assagioli's fourth core concept, the Ideal Model, which we discussed briefly in Chapter I. Here we will attempt an overview and examine a few practical applications. We may wonder why out of the many techniques discussed in *Psychosynthesis*, Assagioli considered the Ideal Model so important. Our opening quote tells us the answer. The Ideal Model is more than a technique: it is the goal of psychosynthesis itself.

The Ideal Model is the client's "image of himself as he can and eventually will be, when the psychosynthesis is achieved." (Assagioli, 1975, p. 164) It is a technique we apply when we have reached the third and fourth phase of the therapy, which Assagioli defines as:

3. Realization of One's True Self – The Discovery or Creation of a Unifying Centre.

4. Psychosynthesis: The Formation or Reconstruction of the Personality Around the New Centre (1975, p. 21)

The Ideal Model continues our work with the will. It helps our clients to centre themselves and define a goal for their psychosynthesis. This goal can be expressed using an inner or external image of what they want to realize. Work with the Ideal Model concerns the will's ability to use the imagination to achieve its goals. The will's task is to regulate and direct the other psychological functions. The trick is to gather motivation, excitement and vitality behind an aim. The will does this via the psychological laws Assagioli defines in *The Act of Will*. In this connection, the two most important of these are:

I. *"Images or mental pictures and ideas tend to produce the physical conditions and the external acts that correspond to them."* (1974 p. 50)

II: *"Attitudes, movements, and actions tend to evoke corresponding images and ideas; these, in turn (according to the next law) evoke or intensify corresponding emotions and feelings."* (1974, p. 51)

As our sessions progressed Maja's image of her inner dignified woman became stronger. Sitting in the chair of the "dignified woman," she could deepen and adjust this image. She saw herself standing in a large room full of people at an important ceremony. She was wearing a bright red evening gown, and beamed with dignity and grace. It was this image of her Ideal Model that she turned into a screen saver on her computer. It became a kind of advert for her Ideal Model. Even more useful was the guided Creative Meditation which she recorded on her cell phone and could listen to any time. These are some of the *active* techniques we can use to promote the client's psychosynthesis.

Her Ideal Model focused Maja's desire to find a relationship based on her new sense of self as a woman. The meditation gradually developed her ability to *feel* worthy. As Assagioli says, our ability to act is stimulated by images we can visualise clearly and *feel* strongly about. This is why Visualization and Creative Meditation are so effective in uncovering new psychological qualities and bringing about changes in behaviour.

Will power can be measured by the amount of energy we can mobilize in order to achieve our goals. The energies of the body, feelings, desires, images, thoughts and intuitive ideas form a potent force with which we can achieve much. The power of images to release the will is known in mental training everywhere, from business to elite sports, and can be traced back to the ancient yoga philosophies.

The images we use must of course be authentic. They may arise spontaneously, or emerge gradually as parts of a puzzle. Certain archetypal images have a potency and reach directly to the core of the soul's purpose. These images come from the Superconscious. Here the soul has sowed seeds that the self can discover at the right time. Such images can become the focus of a lifetime of psychosynthesis. We can access them through exercises that connect us to the Superconscious. In my practice I use various guided visualizations:

Up the mountain and the meeting with the wise man/woman. Here I guide the client on a journey that begins at the foot of a beautiful valley and ends at the top of a sacred mountain. Here we meet a wise person who is an image of the client's Ideal Model.

The temple of the soul. In this visualization the client stands in a valley and can see the temple of his soul at the top of a hill. I guide the client to the temple, where there is a magic mirror that shows the client's true self, the mirror image of the client's Ideal Model.

The theatre of the soul. The visualization guides the client from a valley into a sacred place at the heart of a bright and open forest. Here the soul's theatre is located. The client is guided in and onto the director's chair. Behind the curtain the client can hear the sound and mood of all her subpersonalities. At this point the client asks for the subpersonality that is the truest representation of her Ideal Model to appear on the stage so they can have a dialogue.

In his excellent book 'What We May Be' (1982) Piero Ferrucci provided many examples of how visualizations can be used in psychotherapy. I highly recommend referring to them.

The Ideal Model can be an image of oneself in a specific situation, or an image of someone else who has the qualities you desire (Buddha, Christ, Virgin Mary, etc.). It can also be a symbol i.e. an animal, a flame, a star. We will look more closely at these symbols later.

For several years I worked with an Ideal Model of myself as a yogi. The archetype came to me spontaneously during a meditation, and the name of the yogi immediately resonated with me. He was sitting in a perfect lotus position underneath a tree in a sacred place. The energy he radiated appealed strongly to my psychological type. At first I was watching the yogi in third person, from the "outside" and I noticed his charisma and qualities. I reflected on his name and his possible life story and what could be motivating his yoga practice. The reflections gave me a range of data, either real experiences or simply useful associations, which helped me to create an image of him as my inner wise person. In that way he became as real as possible in my consciousness. Shortly after I started to feel devotion to Brahman. I only had to think of the name Brahman and I would feel a sense of blissful love and surrender to this transcendent and immanent being that is the cause of the universe. I had not previously experienced such fervent love for a Hindu god, which I now did in connection to the image of my inner yogi. Continuing the meditation I saw again how he interacted with other people. I gained many important insights into my current personality through him.

Sometimes I identified myself with the yogi (first person perspective) and held an image of him in my head or at the heart centre. On other occasions I visualised myself as actually being him. Then I found myself sitting by the Ganges looking out over the river of life. When I did this visualisation I would play Indian ragas and burn incense in order to intensify the atmosphere. The outcome of these meditations was contact with the qualities the yogi represented, and an identification with his function. It gave me an inner motivation to teach meditation and spiritual psychology, because now it was the most natural thing in the world to me.

I also visualised myself radiating wisdom and love out to my network of friends and students, and in this way I integrated the Ideal Model in all areas of my life. The intention was not to perfectly manifest the yogi's character, but the visualizations gradually deepened my contact with his qualities and that which he represented. There is no limit to how many variations we can develop once we have found an Ideal Model that works. This yogi is today a living part of my inner world and will always be a subpersonality and archetype that I can draw on when I want to deepen my meditation.

Psychosynthesis is a highly advanced Transpersonal Psychology, because it includes all stages from birth to enlightenment. Not everyone is able or willing to spend so much energy on a visionary quest towards enlightenment. Psychosynthesis, however, does hold this vision alive– the vision of self-actualization and Self-realization – and offers techniques we can use to reach our goal.

VARIOUS TYPES OF SELF MODELS

Our personality rests on previous self-images or models that structure our identity and self-perceptions. These perceptions are formed by the messages and impressions we receive from our environment and our own inherent characteristics. Assagioli describes the unconscious as a large movie archive of exposed images, memories etc. that inform our self-image. However, there are also large amounts of unexposed film that we can consciously influence with our image-making function: the imagination. In Assagioli words, we can discover "the immense reserve of undifferentiated psychic energy latent in every one of us, that is, the plastic part of our unconscious which lies at our disposal, empowering us with an unlimited capacity to learn and to create." (1975, p. 22)

The starting point for the Ideal Model is the receptivity of the unconscious. Through visualizations and Creative Meditation we present the unconscious with images of what we want to be. This is, of course, exactly what the advertising industry does. We buy their products because we are repeatedly exposed to their slogans and images.

Assagioli mentions six different types of self-models that he called false selves, because they do not truly reflect who we really are. They are often in conflict with each other and form subpersonalities and inner voices that compete for our attention. As we will see in the next chapter, it is important that we uncover and transform these false selves in the first and second phase of therapy. Assagioli's (1975, p. 167) six false types are:

1. What we *believe* we are. These models come in two classes where we either *over*-evaluate ourselves or *under*-evaluate ourselves.

2. What we *should like* to be. The idealized and unattainable models.

3. What we *should like to appear* to be to others. There are different models for each of our important interpersonal relationships.

4. The models or images that *others project on us*; that is, the models of what others believe us to be. We are aware of them, but reject them.

5. Images or models that others make of what they *would like us to be*. We are aware of them, but reject them.

6. Images which others *evoke and produce* in us; i.e., images of ourselves evoked by others. We are often unconsciously identified with these.

Number 6 is called "projective identification" and these models can be very damaging. For example, someone brought up in a strict moralising environment that judged them harshly may end up believing that they are "evil".

Assagioli's last category of self-model is the Ideal Model:

7. The Model of that which *we can become*- seen from a realistic perspective.

Another group of self-perceptions form an eighth model. These are the *realistic representations of who we are at our present level of development.*

The Ideal Model uses nature's own design. It is a conscious approach to the creative powers of the unconscious. As Assagioli's says, its essence is to use: "the plastic, creative, dynamic power of images, particular of visual images". (1975, p. 166) An authentic Ideal Model is the embodiment of an idea that originates in the Superconscious, where we can find a number of archetypal ideas of what we may be. These abstract ideas are potent forces that can "incarnate" into a mental-emotional image. This ideal image stimulates the desire and impulse to physical action and realization.

This process has its challenges. The new Ideal Model has to compete against earlier self-images and the conflict between them is a test of our determination to be ourselves. If the resistance is too great, the Ideal Model will not succeed, and the visualization will be abandoned. In such cases we can say that the Ideal Model is stillborn. That is why it is critical to work with both the release *and* transformation of the conflicting self-images that "emerge from the depth" when we start to focus on the Ideal Model. We need to simultaneously redeem *and* transform these conflicting self-images. The work with conflicting subpersonalities happens during the third and fourth stages of the therapy.

Assagioli recommended this approach for transforming resistance: "if, spontaneously, emotions of fear or anger come up, the patient *tries not to fight them*. This is the point: not to fight them, to be permissive, to accept and to experience them. This has to be done over and over again for a sufficient number of times, for in this there is a spontaneous – not forced- freeing of what could be called "psychological allergy"; and after a sufficient number of times the patient without any effort finds himself free from negative emotions." (1975, p. 174)

Maja's conflict related to her inner child, who believed she would be abandoned and ostracized if she expressed her need for intimacy. We therefore worked on Maja's ability to accommodate and meet her inner child's fears, giving it the tender care she had not received in childhood. The Awareness Based approach helped her to observe any bodily and emotional sensations that arose when she visualised making demands on her future boyfriend. The image of the "dignified woman" challenged her "survival personality," the group of self-images and subpersonalities that sought love by being a helper. (This dynamic is described in the chapter on developmental psychology.) When we want to manifest an Ideal Model or other expressions of higher consciousness, we must simultaneously work with the lower unconscious and transform earlier layers of identity formed in childhood.

In some cases, actual people become our role models. Something of this is found in the therapist-client relationship. The psychotherapist can to some extent be a role model in the sense that she/he has *qualities* the client needs to integrate. When the psychotherapist holds the loving space in "mother style" therapy, or acts as supervisor in "father style" therapy, then he/she becomes a model for the clients' ability to father and mother herself. As illustrated in the previous chapter the psychotherapist in this way functions as an external unifying centre for the client. The danger is that the client may become too dependent on the psychotherapist, but our focus on the will reduces this risk considerably. Our work on observation and the objectification of subpersonalities using chair work or creative drawing, also reduces the transference from client to therapist.

Assagioli also refers to *categories* of idols with which a client can be identified

(1975, p. 169). Examples are pop stars, sports figures, rich or "successful" people. These idols can have a powerful influence and if we devote too much attention to them they can stand in the way of an authentic psychosynthesis. Rather than develop our own qualities and resources, we live vicariously through another person's success, whether our children's, a partner's or a celebrity's. Assagioli insists that we view these figures critically, focusing on their unattractive aspects, in order to release the client from possible obsessions.

Maja was fascinated by the married man. He was influential, charismatic and good looking. She suffered from a kind of "tunnel vision," seeing only what fascinated her. Because of this she idealized him. When we started to examine the details of the relationship it became apparent that he had broken many of his promises. He was sexually fascinated by Maja, but his commitment went no further. When I pointed out his hurtful comments and patterns of betrayal, she accepted them intellectually, but her idealization was immune to any critical analysis.

Here disidentification and chair work made a difference. We let her affectionate side occupy a chair in the room and present her case. Her inner teenager *wanted* to be loved by him and was practically obsessed with her romantic transference. The strategy was to transfer her need for love from the man to herself. Maja soon saw that as long as her "inner teenager," and therefore herself, was bound to this man, she would remain stuck in an unhappy love relationship. Through the loving witness and disidentifying, Maja saw how she could contain her inner teenager's pain without becoming identified with it. Breaking out of the relationship would be painful, but we could prepare her to bear the pain, because the alternative was worse. And it was this work that made it possible for Maja to leave the relationship and choose her own path towards a fulfilling love relationship. Her inner teenager eventually welcomed this choice, even if it also feared the breakup.

THE SKILFUL APPLICATION OF THE IDEAL MODEL

When we work with Ideal Models, it is important not to "shoot sparrows with cannons" and introduce idealistic Ideal Models that go far beyond the needs of the client. Most Ideal Models aim at developing specific sides of the client, as witnessed with Maja. Few clients benefit from focusing on an image of their perfect personality too soon in the process. Yet we should not diminish the client's aspirations. If a deep spiritual longing motivates the psychosynthesis, we should meet this with an appropriate Ideal Model.

We often find that our clients' immediate problems are rooted in insufficient development of important qualities such as acceptance, empathy, courage or mental clarity. Identification with negative parental, professional, or gender roles may inhibit their self-esteem. Clearly we must first dissolve negative identifications as much as possible, before working with Ideal Models. Assagioli recommends working with Ideal Models to strengthen insufficiently developed psychological functions (1974, p. 98-99).

In Chapter III, we described how each psychological function constitutes a separate line of development. From this perspective, it is important to develop a model "that represents the next and most urgent step or stage – that of developing an undeveloped psychological function, focussing on a single specified quality or small group of qualities, or abilities which the patient most needs in order to achieve, and even to proceed with, his psychosynthesis." (Assagioli, 1975, p. 170)

There are two kinds of Ideal Models. Some relate to the image of the complete self-actualized or "enlightened" personality. These involve transpersonal psychosynthesis. We can also have more specialized models. Certain types of spiritually oriented people are motivated by very "advanced" Ideal Models. Here we may want to gradually turn the client toward their own perfect ideal and away from a too idealistic choice. We should not do this too suddenly. A client may want to identify with her Buddha-nature and could benefit from an Ideal Model of a wise teacher, which she can seek to realize in practice.

When we work with the Ideal Model we aim to develop the imagination, a psychological function that has significant effect on all the others – as made clear in our earlier discussion about Assagioli's psychological laws. The imagination itself works through synthesis, which is why Assagioli considered it so important. It can operate on the physical, emotional, mental and intuitive levels. We can use our imagination to picture physical objects, or evoke emotional states, to grasp intellectual concepts and contemplate human connectedness. As Assagioli says, training the imagination "is one of the best ways towards a synthesis of the different functions" (Assagioli, 1975, p. 144)

Assagioli particularly emphasized two types of meditation. *Awareness Meditation*, as described in Chapter IV, uses disidentification and self-identification, and an example of this is included in the Appendix. *Creative Meditation* uses visualizations helpful in developing psychological functions. In Awareness Meditation we wake up to the self as pure self-awareness and will. Creative Meditation develops our psychological functions so we can express this self in a liberated personality.

Creative meditation is based on the ability to visualize. In order for us to make our Ideal Model strong enough to compete with the other self-images, we must be able to keep its image in our minds. We do this through visualization. Visualization strengthens our powers of concentration and increases our ability to focus on what is important in our lives. Working with Ideal Models creates greater focus on our authentic personality.

CREATIVE MEDITATION ON THE IDEAL MODEL

Psychosynthesis requires clients to carry on working outside therapy sessions. We can strengthen our client's willingness to do this through using Creative Meditation.

Most spiritual traditions use visualization as part of their contemplative practices. The "power of thought" is well-known in self-development milieus, as is the idea that energy follows thought. We can also say that energy follows imagination. Psychosynthesis is an energy psychology, and Creative Meditation is an important method of mastering our psychological energies.

Creative Meditation draws on the power of visualization. One of the first meditations I practiced was to visualize a sun in my chest radiating transpersonal qualities: acceptance, trust and compassion. During the first decade of my meditation practice, this was my focal point. Visualization creates images in our inner world which contain specific energies. This makes visualisation a powerful tool for harmonizing and synthesising the personality and for aiding the soul's *manifestation* in the world. Visualisation enables the *creation* of a new personality, one through which superconscious energies of the soul can be expressed.

Here are the usual stages of Creative Meditation: Centring, Ascension, Meditation and Anchoring. They show how the Ideal Model can be used as a focal point for visualization.

These steps ensure that our meditation is connected to the highest level of energies available and is free of influences from everyday consciousness. In Centring, before starting the meditation, we direct our awareness towards the Superconscious. Here we go to the symbolic mountain where the meditation begins. Doing this helps to build a clear channel of communication between the self and the soul, as illustrated by the dotted line between these two points in the Egg Diagram. As we strengthen this connection using different types of visualizations our contact with the soul gradually increases. A Creative Meditation included in Appendix describes these stages.

Centring: In this stage we quiet our body, emotions and mind, harmonizing them through the attention of the loving witness. We then assume the role of the observer and ascend the mountain as close to the Superconscious as possible.

Ascension: In this stage we create a channel between the incarnated soul, the self, and the eternal soul or Higher Self.

The ascent begins by anchoring our attention in the heart centre represented by a sun radiating acceptance. This provides "Identity"-strength and allows us to rest in a firm and stabile presence of love. Then, directing our consciousness to the centre of the brain, another, second sun, opens up. Here we make contact with all other awakened souls in the world by expanding our awareness in a 360 degrees radius. We then direct the consciousness from our brain up towards a brilliant sphere of light and love, the seat of the soul. Here we identify with the great being which is the divine Self.

Meditation: We have now reached the meditation stage where the Ideal Model selected as the main focus for the Creative Meditation comes in. We can meditate on anything, only the imagination limits our reach. It may be a good idea to meditate on the qualities we want to strengthen and which are embodied in our Ideal Model. This links our meditation with our life. In Appendix you can find an Ideal Model of *the Lotus of Peace and Harmony*.

Through imagining a brilliant white lotus in the heart centre, emanating peace and harmony, we create an imaginary lotus in the heart, drawing peaceful, harmonious energies from the Superconscious. We create a vehicle through which higher energies can manifest. Anyone who practices Creative Meditation will recognize this. Experienced meditators know the impact of a visualization practice that we come back to. It is like visiting a house you have built, where energies are available the moment you enter.

Through visualization Creative Meditation gradually builds a channel to the Superconscious, home of the higher energies. These energies may begin to enter our everyday life, yet other forces may also appear. Disturbing energies – oppositional forces – and subpersonalities may surface in order to be transformed. This is a natural consequence of meditative work, and is known as "harmony through conflict". When the meditation is over it is time to anchor the energies in the world.

Anchoring: Here we aim for the energies we have gathered to be released into the world. Accumulation of energy can clot our centres producing symptoms of overstimulation: headaches, burning sensations, fatigue, irritability and restlessness. So as we complete each meditation we make the energy available to the world. A very simple way to do it is to pronounce the Hindu syllable OM three times. Each time we visualize the energy flowing out to the world, through our various social and professional networks. The soul wants to bring light to the world. Through pronouncing OM we create a ray of light that uplifts and strengthens the world around us. The creative syllable OM manifests the energies we desire while we pronounce it.

IDEAL MODEL CONNECTING THE SELF AND THE SOUL

The Ideal Model can be the focal point for both personal and transpersonal psychosynthesis. When used in personal psychosynthesis the Ideal Model serves as a focus for personal success. It draws on images that we commonly associate with success, and a particular one is chosen based on the need motivating the work.

The following visualization from Assagioli applies to both personal and transpersonal psychosynthesis: "Picture yourself vividly as being in possession of a strong will; see yourself walking with a firm and determined step, acting in every situation with decision, focused intention, and persistence; see yourself successfully resisting any attempt at intimidation and enticement; visualize yourself as you will be when you have attained inner and outer mastery." (1974, p. 36)

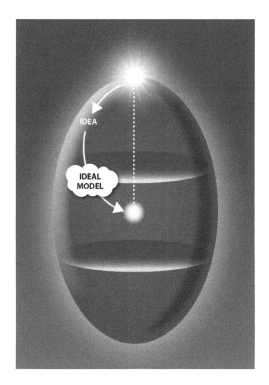

The Ideal Model

When directed towards transpersonal psychosynthesis, the Ideal Model draws on archetypal symbols coming from the Superconscious. Assagioli provides many examples of appropriate symbols (1975, p. 181). Earlier I showed how an image of the sun or a yogi can serve as Ideal Models in Creative Meditation.

These Ideal Models form an indirect link between the self and the soul, different from the direct route via the Bridge of Consciousness. Here the communication comes as an immediate and intuitive certainty, out of "thin air," with no interpretation necessary. I will speak more about this in Chapter X.

This indirect route establishes a bridge between the contents of the Superconscious and our Ideal Model. Archetypes from the Superconscious inspire the Ideal Model; the images of the yogi and sun, for example, both symbolize the archetypal idea of enlightenment. The diagram illustrates how the soul activates an archetypal idea on which the self meditates through the Ideal Model. Assagioli quotes Jung on using symbols as Ideal Models: "the psychological machinery which transmutes energy is the symbol".

Assagioli continues: "there is a great variety of symbols having an anagogic (uplifting) influence that can be made to serve this process, of which ideal human figures or "models" constitute an important class. Two types of these ideal figures, different and in a sense opposite, are respectively suited to men and women. A man may visualize some hero or human-divine Being, such as the Christ, or he can use the image of the ideal woman like Dante's Beatrice or the Madonna. Inversely a woman can take as a model the highest model of womanhood her imagination can conceive or an image of the ideal Man. The influence of such "images" is beautifully expressed in the Indian saying: "Ganga (the sacred river) purifies when seen and touched, but the Holy Ones purify when merely remembered". (1975, p. 275)

I hope it is clear how the Ideal Model can help focus more clearly on our authentic personality. We live in a world full of distractions that constantly demand our energy and attention. The Ideal Model helps us to stay on course. It serves as an inner guidepost, so we as a skilful captain can reach our self-chosen destination safely.

Next we turn to Synthesis: the difficult art of harmonizing, integrating and synthesising the crises, conflicts and obstacles that make up life's journey.

SYNTHESIS
– THE WAY TO FLOW

"Possess thyself and Transform thyself. All psychosynthetic techniques have this as their goal"
(Assagioli, 1983c)

Synthesis is clearly one of the key concepts in Psychosynthesis. We have defined it as a philosophy that sees life as evolving towards unity through the evolution of consciousness. There is an underlying spiritual force behind all that exists, "uniting all beings (some willing but the majority as yet blind and rebellious) with each other through links of love, achieving- slowly and silently, but powerfully and irresistibly- the Supreme Synthesis. " (Assagioli, 1975, p. 31)

In this following quote Assagioli describes the nature of synthesis, the human condition and the path to greater harmony:

"Why is psychosynthesis necessary? "Because all of us have within ourselves different and contrasting psychological elements which alternate and collide. They often reach such a degree of forcefulness as to form separate personalities or subpersonalities which struggle for supremacy within us. This results in a number of contradictions, conflicts, turmoil's and upheavals, which may produce serious nervous difficulties, and often gives the individual a painful and growing sensation of dissatisfaction, instability and disharmony.

But this 'human condition' is by no means fatal and inevitable; we can change and remedy it if we are willing to examine ourselves thoroughly and if we apply the methods that are necessary in order to combine the dissociated and contrasting elements and transform them into a rich and harmonious synthesis.

Synthesis is an organizing and unifying principle which acts in all the kingdoms of nature. We find manifestations of it in inorganic matter in the form of chemical combinations. It acts in a more evident and complicated way in organic life as the power of self-regulation of living bodies, as the delicate and admirable balance between the wear and tear and the rebuilding of tissues.

In the psychological life, the principle of synthesis finds its application in different ways: by unifying opposite vital interests and activities in regard to the outer as well as the inner world of the individual (extraversion and introversion); by synthesizing thought and feeling and other psychological elements around a unifying centre in the psychosynthesis of the personality.

Then there is the problem of spiritual psychosynthesis, that between the personality and the Self or soul, which constitutes the high aim and aspiration of all individuals who cannot be satisfied with terrestrial values only. Another aspect of synthesis is that which unites an individual in numerous relations of integration with other individuals. There is, first of all, the psychosynthesis of the human couple, the eternal problem of the relation between the sexes, about which we shall have more to say further on. Then the synthesis of the family group, of social groups, national groups and, at the very last – as the final ideal – the psychosynthesis of all mankind." (Undated 10)

Synthesis then involves resolving a variety of conflicts:

a. In the personality between different subpersonalities and psychological functions

b. Between the personality and soul

c. In our relationships, family, social groups, nations and humanity as a whole.

Here we will look at the first aspect, that of the personality. This will necessarily involve looking at relationships because it is through them that our subpersonalities often become activated and expressed. In the following chapter I will examine the synthesis of soul and personality.

SYNTHESIS CREATES FLOW

From the perspective of developmental psychology, human beings are faced with numerous inner conflicts between the different needs from the bottom of the Egg-diagram to the top. These can manifest as ambivalence about our different roles and needs: to be a good mother or have an ambitious career; to find security with a man while also being an independent woman; to be uniquely oneself, but also socially accepted. These are just a few examples, but it is the resolution of these and similar conflicts that leads to an integrated and harmonious personality. For this to happen we must first establish contact with the self, which is the organizing centre in the personality. This is our centre of pure self-awareness and will. It is here that we find the resources necessary to actualise our values and act on our needs.

We self-actualize when the aims of the personality are *organized, developed, and directed* into creative, spontaneous and liberated self-expression. This is the goal of personal psychosynthesis. The process of synthesis can be described in another way. We must know who we are and what we want: this is the first stage. We must then realize it in action, using our will and psychological functions. This requires discipline, organization, focus, and the courage to be a self. (Assagioli, 1974, p. 22)

Synthesis develops gradually through the various levels of our personality. A healthy body is a well-regulated organism that maintains its processes without effort as long as its cared for appropriately. We can become sick when we choose a lifestyle that makes the body dependent on unhealthy habits. It is the body's successful synthesis that keeps it alive and well functioning. If we want to use the body as an instrument of the will and other psychological functions, it must be trained accordingly. We must learn how to coordinate our body when we learn to speak, write, move and express ourselves. Likewise with the other psychological functions; they need to be developed so they can cooperate and express their talents.

When a psychological function has been synthesised we can express its qualities freely and easily. Trained dancers can move the body effortlessly. Similarly, if we train our feelings as psychotherapist or actors we can express ourselves empathically and creatively. If we train our mind to think we can express ourselves clearly within our field of knowledge. Synthesis is within reach for all of us, but it is does not arise spontaneously. Disciplined and focused development create the foundation for synthesis, one result of this is "flow".

Flow can be defined as the *spontaneous, effortless expression of an action*. The level of flow depends on the complexity of the action. A ballet dancer's flow is more complex and organized than a child's playful dance. In battle a Kung Fu master will demonstrate an advance degree of development, compared to the violent criminal who spontaneously attacks. They may both fight effortlessly, but the Kung Fu master does so from a higher level of consciousness and perfection.

A requirement of flow is the unification of our psychological functions which makes possible a liberated expression of the will throughout our personality. This demands much effort and work. To achieve what we might call "soul flow," the spontaneous, effortless expression of soulful qualities, such as wisdom, compassion and service, takes a lifetime. Assagioli sees this as the union of the personal and transpersonal and universal will. "The personal will is effortless," Assagioli writes. "It occurs when the wilier is so identified with the Transpersonal Will, or, at a still higher and more inclusive level, with the Universal Will, that his activities are accomplished with free spontaneity, a state in which he feels himself to be a willing channel into and through which powerful energies flow and operate. This is wu-wei, or the "taoistic state," mentioned by Maslow in The Farther Reaches of Human Nature". (1974, p. 20)

In these exalted states being and doing are one. This is the ultimate flow. But even the self-actualized personality will at some point experience conflict between the soul's Transpersonal Will and its own egocentric needs and will. This struggle decides the values that will motivate an individual. According to Assagioli Christ is an example of the highest synthesis. "The most direct and highest statement of the will to unification has been made by Christ: "Not my will, but thine be done," and its achievement is in His triumphant affirmation, "I and the Father are one." (1974, p. 130)

SUBPERSONALITIES– OUR INNER ACTORS

What often stands in the way of synthesis and flow are the inner conflicts that arise between subpersonalities. Assagioli himself did not write much about this conflict, but since his death it has received much attention. In different ways, Rowan (1990), Ferrucci (1982), Sliker (1992), and Rueffler (1995) have elaborated on his theories. In his highly recommended book 'Joyful Evolution' (2011), Gordon Davidson has provided perhaps the most comprehensive description of these subpersonalities.

Assagioli points out that the idea of subpersonalities is not unknown in psychology. For example, William James speaks of "the different selves" and C.G. Jung of personae (1975, p. 71 and 1967b). John Rowan (1990) gives a good overview of the various names they appear under in psychology. Speaking of subpersonalities Assagioli writes:

"It is difficult to realize but each subpersonality that is developed enough to have a will, to be consistent, to think, and to feel, is a miniature personality, and has the same qualities of the general personality. A subpersonality is a small personality on its own that would live in rather deep water. There is the principle of personification, but I will not go into that because it is more theoretical, and I abhor theory. But after all it is not a theory; it is a process of personification. Every psychological element, especially every group of psychological elements, e.g. those that in psychology are called "complexes", tend to personify themselves. Up to this point it is not a theory. We can observe that."

As a simple example let us take the different roles we play in life. A woman often identifies herself with her motherly function to the point that she feels and acts chiefly as a mother. So that is a subpersonality on its own – which may be in conflict with the feminine traits. One of the subjects of practical importance – I don't go into that now – is the conflict between the wife role and the mother role. We may take this up another day, but it shows that each subpersonality has a kind of ego." (Undated 2)

Assagioli sees subpersonalities working in our social roles and also in the different psychological "complexes," inferiority, father, parent, and so on (1975, p. 72-74). Our subpersonalities are expressed in our behaviour and reactions and can be experienced as inner self images or inner voices. As he writes: "Indeed if we observe ourselves, we realize that something is always talking inside us – there are incessant voices from our subpersonalities or from our unconscious, a non-stop inner uproar." (2007, p. 35)

Our personality contains many self-images and inner voices that we have acquired over our lives. They may represent the type of false self we discussed in the chapter on Ideal Models. As social roles they develop in the space between outside influences and our own inner resources and needs. Subpersonalities are related to the different stages of development reviewed in Chapter III.

Our personality is like a large building with several floors. On each floor there are the "actors", each one responsible for the different needs of the floor. We experience these as inner resistance, beliefs, desires and fixed patterns of behaviour. The many needs of our many inner actors can cause much unrest in the building. We can experience our inner actors as energy, moods and vibrations with no particular form, but we can also experience them as people who speak and act in us. The feeling of loneliness, for example, is often attached to a concrete subpersonality, "the lonely", which creates and maintains this mood.

We can experience our actors as the inner child, the teenager, or the adult. These inner actors are self-images we have developed around different roles: mother, father, man, woman, child, brother, sister, profession, etc... When we adopt new functions or social roles we form new and corresponding subpersonalities. They are thus relatively consistent and stable behaviour patterns.

Subpersonalities develop through our *identification* with our roles. If we identify with something for a long time, we create a corresponding inner image with all the psychological qualities associated with the identification. Many informal roles characterize us without our being fully aware of them. If we were bullied at school, we may create a self-image corresponding to this. Our inner child will adopt a victim identity that will shape the child until other experiences alter this, or we work to change it therapeutically.

Roles can also develop based on an identification with *psychological functions* to which we feel attracted. These can be expressed as psychological types: "clown" (imagination), "sceptic" (logic), "hero" (will), "helper" (feeling), "the romantic" (passion), "the practitioner "(sensation), and "dreamer "(intuition).

Age-related roles, that of child, teenager, boyfriend, father, mother, professional and many others all inform us with their own qualities and attitudes. Assagioli stresses the importance of the *psychosynthesis of the ages* in this context. Each stage of development brings important psychological qualities that are necessary for our self-expression. According to Assagioli, the person of an old age can create the psychosynthesis of the ages: "It can be achieved by keeping alive and functioning the best aspects of each age. An older person can consciously re-evoke, resuscitate and cultivate in himself the positive characteristics of all his preceding ages. He can do this by means of various active psychosynthetic techniques such as those based on imagination, suggestion, the Ideal Model, affirmation and meditation. He can further the process by opening himself to the direct influence of persons of the preceding ages, by seeking the company of children, adolescents and the young. But the older person must be willing to participate actively in the life of younger people by playing with them, talking with them, attuning himself to their level." (1983c)

Another group of subpersonalities form around what we can call archetypes. When we identify with them these images from the Collective Unconscious affect us powerfully. Film, literature and other media can create lasting impressions in the unconscious. Children can identify with Pippi, Batman or Snow White, or with dark and demonic images such as the witch, the villain or monster. We can also identify with animals, for example the wolf, the bear or the owl. These archetypes contain potent energies that can affect us for better or worse.

As we've seen, Maja developed an entirely new subpersonality, "the dignified woman," that would contain her gender identity. By meditating on this subpersonality and acting out her character, she gave her life and form. Conversely we also worked with a subpersonality formed of a sense of unworthiness and inadequacy. In one session, Maja contemplated her feeling of unworthiness, and a very dark subpersonality appeared. She explored a woman living alone in a small, miserable apartment, an outcast with shabby clothes. Maja sensed deep shame around her.

This woman spoke of a lonely marriage to a cold emotionless man, and how she had been caught in adultery. The woman identified completely with the rejection and condemnation she received. Maja's empathy with the woman released waves of pain and she experienced a catharsis. Maja interpreted this woman as an archetypal symbol of her inner unworthiness. The "fallen woman" is an archetypal figure who lives in many women unconsciously, often passed down from mother to daughter. Through our work Maja disidentified from the feeling of unworthiness.

She was relieved when she could talk about the "fallen woman" without identifying with her. Her healing began by compassionately attending to her inner fallen woman from the place of the loving witness.

A third category of subpersonalities are created through our relationships with other people.

We can deduce much from what we have looked at here. We've seen that our different developmental stages create various subpersonalities. But we have also seen how we can internalize our most important relationships – parents, siblings, lovers, and friends – and create subpersonalities through them. In psychoanalytical literature this internalising is called object relations and is understood to help children feel safe when their parents are not present. When, as described in Chapter V, Assagioli refers to the psychotherapist as an External Unifying Centre, he is talking about the same function because the outer psychotherapist becomes internalised in the psychological environment of the client. A client's "inner psychotherapist" can be a wise and empathetic inner voice, helping the client through different life situations. This is particularly the case with parental roles that over time become internalised in the child. These powerful subpersonalities will act in us as independent beings *assuming the same roles and values as our external parents.*

Based on observation we see that our subpersonalities act as "living beings." They exist in us, but only as long as we are identified with them unconsciously or consciously. They become more alive in us whenever we repeat their behavioural traits thereby giving them more energy and life.

It may sound strange that our psychological life is so diverse and complex. But Assagioli does not speak symbolically when talking of subpersonalities. "Ordinary people shift from one to the other without clear awareness, and only a thin thread of memory connects them; but for all practical purposes they are different beings – they act differently, they show very different traits." (1975, p. 75) In *Training of the Will* Assagioli describes how:

"Ideas, images, emotions, feelings and drives combine and group themselves, forming "psychological complexes". Thus psychological groupings are created which may grow to the point of becoming actual "subpersonalities", having a semi-independent life. They develop as the various "selves" described by William James (the family self—the professional self—the social self)." (Undated 12)

The Egg-Diagram and Subpersonalities

In the *Act of Will* Assagioli writes that: "All the various functions, and their manifold combinations in complexes and subpersonalities, adopt means of achieving, their aims without our awareness, and independently of, and even against, our conscious will." (1974, p. 57) It's no wonder that we can have difficulty controlling our reactions when a multitude of inner voices are trying for control of our lives. Assagioli also describes how subpersonalities work in the unconscious and are expressed through our dreams. (2007, p. 53)

The chart showing subpersonalities in the various regions of the Egg Diagram illustrates this. The subpersonalities move and shift position in the field of consciousness when we identify with the roles they represent. As Assagioli says, each subpersonality is "able to "rise" or "descend" during the activity in which it is engaged." (Assagioli, 1983c)

It is important to remember that our outer relationships become inner realities. This means, for example, that we all have an image of our parental figure *inside* us, and that it is trying to maintain our parents' norms and values. When we hear our parents' voice inside our head, it is our inner image of them speaking.

Subpersonalities have a life of their own, but they are also stuck in a time warp. They are often caught in the time in our lives when they were created. Our past is their present and they act out their lives in our life, just below the threshold of consciousness. Some of them evolve naturally through life circumstances, but others are stuck in the past.

The last and perhaps controversial category of subpersonalities are those related to reincarnation. When meditating on moods connected to a subpersonality some clients feel they are in contact with a past life. The "fallen woman" Maja encountered, for example, could be interpreted by another person as someone they were in a past life. It is up to the individual to interpret subpersonalities as an archetype or a previous life. The fact remains that ideas of past lives frequently pop up in sessions and we can interpret these subpersonalities as previous selves still active in our present incarnation.

To conclude let me mention that subpersonalities appear only in the Lower and Middle Unconscious. Only on the level of the mental, emotional and physical can these energies come into form. At the level of the Superconscious energies are formless. We experience them as light phenomena, inspiration and energy rather than actual images or thought forms.

THE DEVELOPMENT OF SUBPERSONALITIES

Subpersonalities develop naturally in all of us as a response to the challenges of life. New relationships, work, and responsibilities forces us to learn new roles or develop existing ones, and in the process new subpersonalities are formed or existing ones are developed. This can lead to conflict between new demands and our ability to meet them.

Our development does not necessarily progress in a slow "natural" pace through one crisis or conflict to another. It is a gruelling business where we live out our subpersonalities through our projections. When through disidentification we withdraw our projections, we no longer live out these inner conflicts in the outer world. We discover that the outer world is a kind of mirror reflecting the subpersonalities we contain. Our reactions are our subpersonalities in action. We realize it is more important to change ourselves rather than others. We understand why we should remove the log that is on our own eyes and not worry so much about the speck in our brother's.

Assagioli suggests that we develop our subpersonalities by looking at life as a play. "The starting point", he writes, "is the complete immersion in each subpersonality… The goal is the freed self, the I consciousness, who can play consciously various roles." (1975, p. 75) When we act the role of mother, woman or teacher, and bring our values, resources and personal qualities into this role, the role becomes authentic. When we also realise that we are not the role, we experience greater freedom in relation to the role and "the less we are identified with a particular role, the better we play it". (Assagioli, 1975, p. 75)

Assagioli's description of the optimum relationship between the soul, the self and subpersonalities (1983c) can be expressed most usefully using metaphors. These metaphors are valuable tools in therapy and I use them all in my practice. I adjust them to the needs of the client and they are a good example of the educational aspect of Psychosynthesis. The psychotherapist is not only a healer, but also a guide or teacher.

I use the following metaphors for the relationship between the soul, the self and subpersonalities:

The Writer, Director and Actors
The Captain, the Sailing Master and the Sailors
The Board, the Director and Staff
The Composer, the Conductor and the Musicians.

The soul is the *inspiring* force that contains the bigger picture, communicates meaning and provides the overall purpose. Useful metaphors are the Author, Captain, Board and Composer.

The self is the *guiding force*, organizing and coordinating the work between subpersonalities. It also facilitates the work of development. The metaphors Director, Sailing Master, Director and Conductor belong here.

Subpersonalities are the *executive function*. They use their talents and skills to bring the work to life. Here we use the metaphors of the Actors, Sailors, Staff and Musicians.

This cooperation is often lacking. Our connection to soul is usually weak and we lack a clear sense of meaning and purpose. Or the personality may not be adequately integrated and so the self is unable to coordinate and manage the various subpersonalities. This is very often the case. The inner house is divided against itself, and we waste energy attending to our subpersonalities' conflicting needs. It also happens that subpersonalities simply don't have the skills to carry out the plans of the Board (the soul) and the Director (self). Whatever the cause the consequence is conflict and an inability to realize our needs.

When we discover our subpersonalities, we also, paradoxically, discover the self. Assagioli writes that: "Revealing the different roles, traits etc., emphasizes the reality of the observing self. During and after this assessment of the subpersonalities one realizes that the observing self is none of them, but something or somebody different from each. This is a very important realization and another of the keys for the desired future". (1975, p. 76)

This process brings subpersonalities under the self's loving governance and leads to the synthesis of the personality. Assagioli suggests the following stages (1983c):

First, the discovery of the many aspects of the personality through disidentification. This requires the realization of the self as a centre of pure self-awareness and will.

"The second phase," Assagioli writes, "is that in which the existing subpersonalities are transformed and trained by the "director". This presupposes a clear and stable self-consciousness, the employment of a firm and decisive will, and a constant sense of self-awareness, both as subject and, at the same time, as agent." (1983c)

The synthesis of subpersonalities implies the release of a "complex", a painful life theme (loneliness, anxiety etc.) by applying its positive potentials and energies. Serious life issues require working with several subpersonalities over a long time. The interaction between groups of subpersonalities is necessary and usually proceeds through five stages. Subpersonalities must be *recognized, accepted, transformed, integrated and synthesized*. These phases may be understood as follows[12]:

Acknowledgement requires us to disidentify with the subpersonality, creating the initial freedom from it. The subpersonality is seen, and through disidentifying with it, we transcend it. It is then possible to observe the subpersonality as an object in our consciousness.

Acceptance activates love. The subpersonality can now be held with love and empathy. This softens its defence mechanisms and a loving relationship between observer and subpersonality becomes possible. We grasp the subpersonality's primary need (its cause). The Self is now immanent, present in the subpersonality as empathic consciousness.

Transformation brings creativity into play. Through dialogue and visualization we discover the transpersonal potential of the subpersonality, its inner light.

Integration involves work with the will. Our subpersonalities' primary needs for security, love, status, freedom etc. are met by finding ways to accommodate them in our lives.

---

12 Jim Vargui, 1974, gives his perspective on the stages in his article, even if the example used is very optimistic.

Synthesis is the result of a long-term effort where groups of subpersonalities are included, transformed and integrated. Where we were previously blocked the way is open. We experience flow and a spontaneous ability to be our self. Our subpersonalities are in flow under the guidance of the self.

THE PRACTICAL WORK WITH SUBPERSONALITIES

We can apply many methods in our work with subpersonalities. We have already mentioned chair work, and here we emphasize the client's chair. This is the chair of the self, who lovingly observes and directs the subpersonalities. Subpersonalities are given their own chairs and a subpersonality is given a voice when the client sits in the chair dedicated to it. The chair of the soul can be anywhere in the room, but often I ask the client to stand up honestly with her hand on her heart and look out over the chairs. Standing symbolizes the transcendent and the hand on the heart represents the immanent perspective. Important insights can come from this.

Creative drawing is also effective in identifying and releasing the energies of subpersonalities. Choice of colours and shapes gives great insight here. We ask the client to draw the subpersonality or its mood, without thinking too much. This helps the client to disidentify and he can tune in to different aspects of the problem by examining the effect of colour.

Guided visualization is in my view one of the most effective way to work with subpersonalities. For this the client must be able to observe his inner states. We must be able to see inner images of our subpersonalities but to be able to feel and express them is also quite central. Inspired by Gordon Davidson's work, my friend and colleague Søren Hauge and I have developed a method we call SoulFlow. In SoulFlow we take a subpersonality through the stages of recognition, acceptance, transformation, integration and synthesis. In the Appendix I have included an outline of the process.

Let me end this chapter with an example of how Soul Flow works in practice, showing how some of the principles we've mentioned can be applied therapeutically.

In a session with Maja we created a SoulFlow with her "fallen woman" (see Appendix).

We created a healing pillar which opened a loving field of awareness where the transformational work could happen. The healing pillar represents the space where the soul and the unconscious are connected to the self as a loving witness.

It is also an exercise where the client learns how to create a loving space for himself by opening his heart to all that his personality contains.

With closed eyes and in a meditative state, the client asks the relevant subpersonality to inwardly come forward. Maja already had an image of the fallen woman and could easily picture her. Here it is important to relate to the subpersonality as a *living being*, with unconditional acceptance of her emotional state. Soul Flow is a radically appreciative approach where any destructive traits in the subpersonality are interpreted as a survival strategy because it has not been met and seen in love. The subpersonality is now being recognized and the next stage is acceptance.

At this stage I asked Maja to tell her "fallen woman" that she is a *living* and valued part of her unconscious. Maja told her subpersonality that she wants to hear her story and understand what she needs. Maja listened and held the pain and despair. At one point Maja broke down in tears and struggled to stay focused. I gently reminded her that she is the loving witness and must hold the inner space for her subpersonality. This helped Maja disidentify from the pain so she could send it love. We spent some time understanding how her subpersonality had identified with condemnation, with what had led her to be unfaithful, and the consequences of rejection. Maja practiced being a good mother – a warm empathetic person for her own wounded parts. This is the first step in the transformative phase.

When the pain had been met and redeemed, I asked Maja to inform "the fallen woman" that she is stuck in the past. Maja told her that she now lives in Denmark and visualized an image of her present life. When she learned that her reality no longer exists she became puzzled and surprised. The subpersonality awoke as from a dream; this often has a powerful effect. This reality check is important because it allows the subpersonality to disidentify. Maja told the fallen woman how infidelity is viewed from a more modern and tolerant perspective and this certainly had an influence on her. This is the second stage of the transformative phase.

Assagioli says that subpersonalities can be considered as reflections of both the self and the soul (Undated 2). They have the same qualities as the personality but in order for the subpersonalities to reflect the soul they must discover their own light. The soul is immanently present in the personality through its radiance but the personality must be able to reflect this radiance. This is possible only if they discover their own light. I therefore asked Maja to tell the fallen woman that she also has a light in her heart, just as Maja herself has. Maja asked the woman to recognize her light, and together they explored its *qualities*. This is important for the subpersonality and therefore also for Maja. There were tears of joy. The light was full of beauty, harmony and aesthetic sense. The appearance of the fallen woman changed dramatically, becoming much more like Maja's Ideal Model. She radiated dignity and grace. This made such an impression on Maja that she spontaneously renames the woman "Grace". This is the third transformative phase.

The next stage is to integrate Grace's into Maja's heart. Maja told Grace that there is a place in the heart that contains everyone she loves. Maja invited Grace into the heart space, and Grace accepted the invitation. A feeling of flow accompanied her exit from the dark regions of the unconscious and entrance into the heart space of light. Maja visualized more images of her new life and told Grace that her goal is to meet someone with whom she can have a nurturing and equal love relationship. The arrangement works as a team. Grace understood that she plays a significant role in Maja's life. This is the integrative phase.

This session was a turning point for the Maja. She was now able to *feel* the dignity of her inner woman. She now had positive images of herself, which could inspire and guide her in different situations. She had not yet achieved her aim to freely and spontaneously express her dignity but she had taken an important step toward it.

We see how important work with subpersonalities can be. It is one way in which the soul incarnates with its superconscious qualities in the unconscious. When the lower unconscious reflects the qualities of the Superconscious, the soul has a real presence in the personality. In the next chapter we will take a look at the qualities of the Superconscious and how we can reap from its abundance.

1) The Lower Unconscious
2) The Middle Unconscious
3) The Superconscious
4) The Field of Consciousness
5) The self and the observer
6) The Soul
7) The Collective Unconscious
8) The Bridge of Consciousness

THE SUPERCONSCIOUS
– THE WAY TO ABUNDANCE

"What distinguishes Psychosynthesis from many other attempts at psychological understanding is the position that we take as to the existence of a spiritual Self and of a superconscious, which are as basic as the instinctive energies described so well by Freud."
(Assagioli, 1975, p. 193)

The Superconscious, or the Higher Unconscious, is Assagioli's 6th core concept. Aside from the will, he has probably written more about the Superconscious than any other topic. In *Transpersonal Development,* published thirteen years after his death in 1974, he explores in great detail transpersonal states and how we can connect to them.

Earlier we defined the Superconscious as the collected energies that expand our consciousness from the personal to the transpersonal. Many people have testified to experiencing a powerful sense of belonging to or being "at one with" the planet, humanity or existence itself. All truly original scientific, artistic, technological, psychological and cultural innovations have their source in the Superconscious. These are the ideas that push humanity up the evolutionary ladder. These heightened states of consciousness give hope for a world of peace and harmony. Through the Superconscious we experience the unity of nature and man, an understanding that can save both from destruction. This is why it is important to develop our Higher Consciousness. As Assagioli writes:

"One of the greatest causes of suffering and misguided action is fear. This can be individual anxiety or the collective fear which can carry a nation into war. The experience of the superconscious reality does away with fear, for any sense of fear is incompatible with a realization of the fullness and permanence of life. Another cause of error and wrong conduct is the urge to fight which stems from the ideas of separation, from aggression, and from feelings of hostility and hatred. In the calm atmosphere of the superconscious such feelings cannot exists. Anyone whose consciousness has been enlarged, who feels a sense of participation, a sense of unity with all beings, can no longer fight. It seems absurd: it would be like fighting oneself! In this way, the most serious of problems. The ones causing the greatest distress, are resolved or eliminated by the development, enlarging and ascent of the consciousness to the level of Higher Reality. " (2007, p. 25-26)

The Superconscious is our doorway to the spiritual, but what is *spirituality*?

Psychosynthesis distinguishes between the "normal" consciousness of the Lower and Middle Unconscious and the transpersonal energies of the Superconscious. This division helps us distinguish between the egocentric and the altruistic. This differ-ence is essential because it is through the Superconscious that we can help solve the most fundamental human problems. Psychosynthesis aims for a world of harmony and peace, but this can only come about through our own will-to-synthesis. So we must start with ourselves. The Superconscious provides us with the energy to build bridges of understanding and harmony, in ourselves and the world.

Yet our own inner lives contain forces that divide us and lead to conflict. As As-sagioli remarked: "Selfishness constitutes the fundamental obstacle. Selfishness springs from the desire to possess and to dominate, which is an expression of the basic urges of self-preservation and self-assertion. "(1974, p. 86)

Assertiveness and aggression can cause inner and outer conflict, but we should not condemn or repress them. They are necessary for our survival. Maslow speaks of "deficiency needs." By definition, these are "needs" for something we lack, whether it is as simple as food or a place to live. They must be fulfilled if we are to develop, but we must learn to master and refine them so that we can get along with ourselves and others. Maslow also speaks of "being" or "meta" needs, needs of a *creative* character. Maslow called these *growth* needs. For Assagioli, they arise from the Superconscious, a source of spiritual plenty.

Assagioli defines spirituality in the following way:

"To be spiritual does not mean only to be able to transcend the little self in a "ver-tical" direction through realisation of the Self and communion with the Supreme Reality. It includes also a "horizontal" attitude, that is, communion of thought and love and harmonious collaboration with all fellow-creatures. This expansion is achieved through "concentric circles," which gradually include ever larger groups, from the family to humanity as a whole. " (Undated 1)

Ken Wilber describes how moral development follows four stages, in line with Assagioli's concentric circles. Moral development in this context refers to care and concern, from individual concern only extending as far as "me" and "mine" to concern for all people. Wilber refers to his theory as *the spiral of compassion* and he bases it on the research of Lawrence Kohlberg and Carol Gilligan (Wilber, 2000d). Here the scope of the self widens from self-centric care (me) to ethno-centric care (us), the world-centric care (all peoples and beings) to cosmo-centric care (all). The first two stages include ourselves and the people we like, love and depend on. At the world-centric stage consciousness expands to identify with humanity. Here the transpersonal field begins, with its holistic vision of humanity as one. The idea of human rights and the motivation for many humanitarian movements emerge from this stage, but to believe in these things is clearly not the same as practicing them in everyday life.

Assagioli agrees that spirituality requires the practice of high ethical standards: "All claims of spirituality have to be expressed through a more pure strict and conscious morality than average man ...You shall know the tree by its fruits. "Moral purification is the key to understanding the true reason for the long pilgrimage through the inner worlds. "(2007, p. 154) In order to practice a world-centric morality, we must identify with higher values. Assagioli defines spirituality as: "all the functions and activities which have as common denominator the possession of values higher than the average, values such as the ethical, the aesthetic, the heroic, the humanitarian and the altruistic." (1975, p. 38)

Transpersonal Consciousness makes us idealists in the broadest sense of the term. Transpersonal psychosynthesis works not "for the purpose of withdrawal but for the purpose of being able to perform more effective service in the world of men." (Assagioli, 1975, p. 210)

THE SUPERCONSCIOUS IN PSYCHOTHERAPY

In therapy, it is important to be able to help clients through a spiritual awakening and related crises. Assagioli suggests four types of spiritual crises that could be confused with "normal" ones, because they appear with similar symptoms.

1. Crisis Preceding the Spiritual Awakening

2. Crisis Caused by the Spiritual Awakening

3. Reactions to the Spiritual Awakening

4. Phases of the Process of Transformation (1975, p. 40)

In order to understand these crises, we must distinguish between two types of people and two types of problems. Assagioli differentiates between people who have an ideal of being "normal" and others who no longer can adjust to normality. (1975, p. 54) The first type might have psychological scars from a difficult upbringing, which has caused problems with their relations to other people. They have not been able to experience a harmonious integration to normality. This type needs to secure a good, stable life so their basic social needs can be met. In these cases personal psychosynthesis is the aim and talk about Higher Consciousness would not be useful.

The second group have faced an existential crisis and adjusting to "normal" society will not help them. Their quest for meaning and purpose and indifference to "normal" values is often met with surprise or outright rejection. They have woken up to values beyond the normal. They want to know: What is the meaning of my life? How do I live my "calling"? How do I become the best version of me?" They have the same "deficiency" needs as everyone else, but fulfilling these is no longer the centre of their lives.

Although, as Assagioli says, "an individual may have genuine spiritual experiences without being at all integrated, i.e. without having developed a well-organized, harmonious personality"(Assagioli, 1961), it is clear that transpersonal work often requires personal development, in order to consolidate transpersonal experiences.

Yet it is important to distinguish between the two types of problems. It is not appropriate to open up to superconscious energies in guided visualization if clients have a weak ego structure. They do not have the necessary cognitive and emotional maturity to handle energies that expand the boundaries of the personality. They first need to establish healthy and firm ego boundaries, to learn how to say "no" and to become aware of personal needs. These clients often cannot observe their experiences and so cannot easily disidentify. Long-term "mother" therapy is needed here, until a mature personality gradually emerges.

There are, of course, many exceptions to the above, as the example of Maja shows. She wanted to develop her identity as a woman, and very few transpersonal aspects were involved. She was successful, intelligent, and had a relatively harmonious social life. We focused on improving her self-love and femininity. Had she wanted therapy that focused on shared idealistic values, the transpersonal would have come in. But this was not so with Maja. She was philosophical but rather conventional. She wanted to meet a good man she could start a family with and who could also be her best friend and lover. She still had a sense of an inner space of love and wisdom, which we called "the voice of the soul". I asked her to stand in the room as the soul, overlooking the chairs representing various subpersonalities. I asked her to put the right hand on her heart, and to tell me what was emerging in her life. What kind of woman did she want to be? This exercise has transpersonal elements, but its *intention* was personal.

Let's look briefly at the four spiritual crises and see how we can guide the client through them.

1. CRISIS PRECEDING THE SPIRITUAL AWAKENING

People interested in transpersonal perspectives have at some point experienced this type of crisis. Assagioli uses Viktor Frankl's term *existential vacuum* to describe this condition (1974, p. 106). Needs associated with normality no longer makes sense as a primary motivator and there is a yearning for something different. Often a sense of boredom, depression and despair, a sense of a lack of direction in life, precipitates the crisis. These symptoms may seem familiar and normal, but the need behind the crisis is very different. It is a need for meaning, to somehow make a difference in the world. The heart has been opened and a clear humanitarian motivation emerges. The call to service is a sure sign that the client is becoming conscious of the soul.

Here the therapist mirrors back the client's longing with acceptance and appreciation. His symptoms are the growing pains of an emerging new consciousness.

A conflict between the needs of the personality and the soul may arise. The soul may urge the client to find a new and more meaningful job, but the personality may balk at taking the plunge for a number of reasons, financial, loss of status, ostracism. Here it is crucial that the psychotherapist understands the client's spiritual process. Knowing that she is undergoing a natural development, and that the psychotherapist has gone through the same process, encourages the client to "follow the heart" and carry on.

Transpersonal exercises are a great help in clarifying the spiritual longing. Visualizations can guide clients to the temple of the soul, where their longing can be heard and seen more clearly. The client can also be guided up a mountain where a talk with a wise person can provide meaningful perspectives. There are many examples of this in the Psychosynthesis literature; Assagioli (1975), Ferrucci (1982, 2014) and Schaub (2013) are particularly useful. The main idea at this point is to help the client develop a new vision of life, activate the will and manage the inner resistance to change.

Sometimes clients know exactly what they want, but simply can't bring it about. Psychological functions, perhaps the will, may be undeveloped. The knowledge, passion or imagination to realize the dream is missing. Here the focus will be to develop the weaker functions. With Maja it was the feeling function. We focused on redeeming the pain she had accumulated, which helped her to be present with her emotions. When the will supports a client's vision and she seeks to live it, new demands arise. She exits her comfort zone and enters a new landscape, which requires new skills, which hitherto have been dormant. Yet the meaning and authenticity one finds there are worth the effort.

2. CRISIS CAUSED BY THE SPIRITUAL AWAKENING

There are different ways of managing these crises; here I will look at only a few general themes. One is how the personality reacts to the new spiritual energies. For an unprepared personality, new values and energies of higher consciousness may be overwhelming. Clients may have "seen the light" or had a "revelation," and this can manifest in different ways, depending on the psychological type.

One type of reaction is *ego inflation*. Here clients identify with the transpersonal energy and may feel called to a special and important mission. They are not aware of the difference between the potential and the actualization; they may have felt the power, but are not able to manifest it properly. I once worked with a woman who held a leading position in the educational sector. She believed her mission was to reform the educational system because she had the right ideas. But after many rejections she was close to losing her job because she couldn't cooperate with other people. She was inspired and motivated, but a fanatical single-mindedness made it impossible for her to work with anyone else. She felt victimised, misunderstood and not seen. Her need for self-assertion hijacked the ideas that originated from the transpersonal realm; this did neither she nor the ideas any good.

Other types may become inflated with love. This may result in a relationship with a spiritual teacher that knows no boundaries. They are often motivated by a great love of the spiritual, which they want to express in a relationship. The *idea* of a great spiritual romance can become an obsession and any signs of failure bring enormous frustration. This type lacks grounding; their ideals are difficult to realise because their feeling of love is too strong. I worked with a man who was a dry technical type, trained as an engineer. He had fallen in love with a woman who was "alternative" and lived in a spiritual community. She read his astrological chart and introduced him to idealistic passions he never experienced before. Together with her he wanted to provide clean drinking water to developing countries. She did not reciprocate his feelings, but wanted them to be friends and to support him in realising his idealistic vision. His feeling function was undeveloped and his romantic idealization of the woman hijacked his initial transpersonal ideas.

These examples show the need for a wise and balanced approach in psychotherapy. Often we cannot deal with the problem from a purely rational perspective. We must find an appropriate outlet for these energies so they do not swamp the personality. Meet the good intention but encourage its realistic expression: that is the task. It is useful to focus the will on the positive aspects of the vision; then the client can realize it through clarifying his purposes, values and planning, followed by practical actions.

Sorting out any subpersonalities awakened in the process is recommended in order to uncover any underlying motivations and reactions. Often the client will understand the needs that drive them. A transpersonal state and an inner child, each fighting for attention, can often lead to confusion.

Opening the client up to new visions is not recommended at this stage. Their present challenges are demanding enough. But it is crucial to strengthen the loving observer. A transpersonal opening requires a strong centre, capable of managing the unfamiliar energies. This centre is the self, and the client must learn to disidentify from the transpersonal energies, otherwise he will suffer over-stimulation. These are the kinds of problems that come from identifying with only one level of our inner house, without including the others.

3. REACTIONS TO THE SPIRITUAL AWAKENING

The soul and the personality's "honeymoon" ends when the demands of everyday reality kick in. Even with all the exciting and inspiring new visions, the personality itself has not changed. The new energies place new demands on one's ethics and behaviour. Assagioli says: "Sometimes it even happens that lower propensities and drives, hitherto lying dormant in the unconscious, are vitalized by the inrush of higher energy, or stirred into a fury of opposition by the consecration of the awakening man – a fact which constitutes a challenge and a menace to their uncontrolled expression." (1975, p. 47)

Clients may feel they've taken the wrong direction because their reactions have become more intense. It is as if they have fallen from a mountaintop with a beautiful view, back down to grim reality. Anger, exhaustion, sadness and feelings of inferiority are common. This is sometimes called the "crisis of duality," because one is torn between the ideal and everyday self.

When we meet the client at this stage, we need to focus on the awakening of the heart. After a glimpse of the nature of the soul, they can easily become self-critical and judge themselves too harshly. An idealized version of themselves with which they are identified can become a harsh inner critic. Here the Superego hijacks the transpersonal energies and demands perfection. The client needs to understand that the pronouncements of this inner voice are the exact opposite of spiritual development. Only a poverty stricken love can love only what is perfect. By containing, accepting and loving the imperfect the heart raises it to a higher level. Love breeds love. At this stage the therapist must hold the loving space for the client and be the wise teacher who understands the process of awakening, because she has lived through it. Here we help the client relive the transpersonal experiences of pure being, depth and authenticity while transforming the painful inner states.

The therapist's presence can bring healing and loving acceptance to the pain. The client learns how to observe, accept, breathe through and let the pain go. He learns to trust his will-to-be-a-self and meets the challenges of life. This may cause people unaccustomed to this new version of the client some dismay. It also helps to work with subpersonalities in the client's subconscious, who now must learn to express themselves at a higher level.

Significant shifts in the client's outer life may also occur. Old relationships end, and new ones develop. Life may seem confusing and chaotic because one has a foot in each camp: the old life no longer makes sense, but the new one is not yet clear. There may be more harmonious passages through this crisis, but they are rare in clinical practice. This stage leads to the next, where the client learns how to pursue a spiritual practice in life.

4. PHASES OF THE PROCESS OF TRANSFORMATION

Waking up to the soul has its price: the transformation and refinement of the personality. Assagioli calls this "the way of purification" and in it old behaviour patterns are purged. A kind of moral awakening accompanies the values of the heart. We begin to act on the interest of the whole and not only our personal affairs. Challenges may arise regarding intimacy, money and power. An intimacy of the heart, enjoying greater sensitivity and empathy may curb selfishness in relationships. Conscience speaks and we reject being exploited or exploiting others. Ethical issues concerning how we earn and spend money may arise. Our consumer habits are scrutinised in the light of our conscience. Our new connection to the world makes us consider how we consume its resources. The soul wants to influence the world and this includes the place of power in our relationships. Waking up to the soul's values, we feel the continuous inner pressure of the Transpersonal Will. It is a living force pushing us beyond our comfort zone. It insists that we grow and become greater. Its persistent appeal is that we give more love, strength and creativity to the world. The soul's main motive is service.

This evolutionary pressure meets resistance in the personality, which reacts with fear and protests against the new demands. Clients at this stage have found "the way", but need help transforming their inner resistance. Work on subpersonalities that resist the will-to-be-self can help. (Chapter VIII.) But we must remember that subpersonalities should be seen as potential "partners" in this work. They possess an inner light, which can mirror superconscious energies. If the soul is the sun, and the Superconscious the sunlight, then subpersonalities are the moon reflecting this light. Assagioli describes it this way:

"The spiritual elements that come down like rays of sunlight into the human personality- into our personal consciousness- and form a link between our ordinary human personality and the Higher Self, the spiritual Reality. They are like rays of light pouring down, taking on various shades of colour and dispersing, depending on the permeability or the transparency of our personal consciousness." (2007, p. 241)

Psychosynthesis aims to *manifest* the Superconscious in the world. This means accessing these energies *through* the lower unconscious. We may think that we can rise above the lower unconscious, but we forget that we are functioning *through* the body and its nervous system which operate at a lower frequency than the Lower Unconscious.

Transpersonal energies are rays of light, that is, qualities that when integrated into the personality refine it. The vision is to learn to interact with the environment spontaneously with love and wisdom. Assagioli describes it this way: "Therefore, we must endeavour to develop, on the one hand sympathy, love, and insight and on the other disinterestedness, self-forgetfulness, and emotional detachment. In this way we shall achieve one of the main purposes of our evolution – a wise love without attachment, a truthful love which gives freedom and makes us free." (1934)

In chapter III we looked at Assagioli's descriptions of our inner worlds, including the upper levels of this energy spectrum. Based on this, I would suggest that the Superconscious contains energies we can call abstract thoughts, and from these emerge scientific, cultural and political *ideas*. There is also an imaginal world of visual impressions, sounds and sensations, which we can call *aesthetic*. Then there

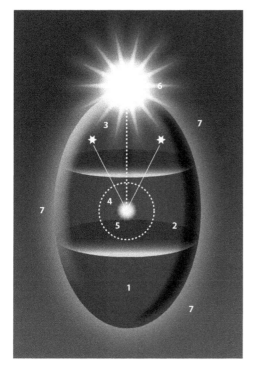

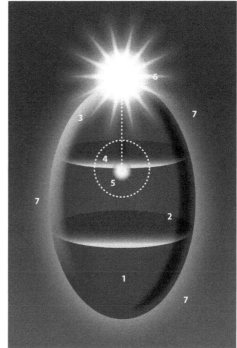

Creative Talents

The ascend of the self

is the world of *intuition*. This shows us how everything is connected and this gives rise to wisdom, ethics and altruism. Heroic and self-sacrificing energies come from the world of the will. These worlds are fields of universal and unifying consciousness; through them we realize that everything is connected. They are impersonal and relate to all humanity and the planet itself. The consciousness experienced in the awakening depends on psychological type. Assagioli uses seven different types, based on the will, love, aesthetics and science etc. (Undated 16, Ferrucci 1990)

Experiencing these energies does not mean that we automatically develop a transpersonal value system. There are many examples of how these impressions can be used selfishly. In the 'Creative Talents' diagram Assagioli shows how someone can access transpersonal elements, while his consciousness is still centred in the personality (1975, p. 201). Mozart was clearly a genius, but his personality was immature. We've spoken of this in Chapter III in respect to the different developmental lines. Here we find people who have an obvious creative talent. They bring something completely new, original and pioneering to the world, but at the same time they are domineering and selfish because of an inflated ego. These are classic examples of how the ego can hijack transpersonal energies by believing and presenting these energies as something unique to individual.

When the developmental line of the self enters the transpersonal, we find the great universal geniuses whose ideas, sensibilities, and spirit have shaped our culture. Assagioli mentions Pythagoras, Plato, Dante, Leonardo da Vinci and Einstein. He created the chart 'The Ascent of the Self' to illustrate this idea. (1975, p. 200). Here the consciousness of the self is permanently connected to the Superconscious. The separate self merges with the universal consciousness and experiences a profound sense of unity with all mankind.

So there is a marked difference between the self that ascends to the Superconscious, which results in an expansion of self-identity, and the self receiving inspirations from the Superconscious without any following expansion of self-identity.

TRANSPERSONAL METHODS

Finally let us look at some methods of expanding our consciousness. A psychotherapist following a spiritual practice will be able to advise clients on a similar journey. It involves three main tasks of transpersonal psychosynthesis and is what Assagioli calls for Self-realization. These 3 tasks are:

a. Purify and refine the personality's reactions to transpersonal energies,

b. Strengthen the capacity to receive the abundance of transpersonal energies that are present in the client's Superconscious.

c. Purifying the channel connecting the self and the soul enabling the clients to awaken to their identity as soul.

There are examples of the first task in Chapter VIII, and we will review the third in the next chapter. We will end this chapter by considering the second task.

Assagioli mentions two categories of exercises:

1. Those which promote the elevation of the "I" or Ego, the centre of self-consciousness, to levels usually superconscious and towards union with the spiritual Self.

2. Those which promote the opening of the consciousness to the "descending" inflow of the contents and energies of the superconscious." (1967b)

In my book *The Call to Greatness* (2012), I described 14 different types of meditation we can use to achieve the above. These are dynamic, sensitive, reflective, observing and creative meditations, aimed at different psychological types and purposes. The book is based on Psychosynthesis and is a guide to transpersonal work and is useful further reading. Here I will focus on the value of developing both the clients' and the psychotherapists' intuition. Assagioli wrote:

"We cannot conceive a true and successful therapist who has not developed and uses the intuition. For this reason, this technique should be given special attention in every didactic psychosynthesis." (1975, p. 221)

As mentioned, intuition is a basic psychological function. Each function provides its own unique insight into reality. Intuition is a function of synthesis because it "considers the totality of a given situation or psychological reality ... directly in its living existence." (Assagioli, 1975, p. 217) Intuition gives us a direct experience of the inner reality or essence of another human being, a situation or an object. "Intuition assimilates the very essence of what the object really is."(2007, p. 63) Assagioli describes it as "the opening of an inner eye which enables us to perceive realities which are not visible to our normal mental sight." (2007, p. 63) Etymologically the word intuition is from in-tueri, which means "to see within".

Intuition is infallible when it is true intuition, and Assagioli distinguishes between everyday sense intuition and transpersonal intuition. The former are gut feelings, sensations and emotions. These intuitions are mixed with our own subjective emotions hence they may or may not be true. Transpersonal intuitions are not necessarily emotional. They are more like entering a room where everything is illuminated and you can understand its *meaning* and purpose at once.

Intuition is essential in our work with psychosynthesis. Assagioli writes: "Only intuition gives true psychological understanding both of oneself and of others. Whenever one wants to reach a true understanding of the essence of the specific quality of a human being, of a group, or of human relationships, the use of intuition is indicated and even necessary. " (1975, p. 220-221)

To strengthen our intuition we must clear the way for it. We must cultivate stillness and disidentify with the content of consciousness. This quiets the personality and makes it receptive. Troubled thoughts, feelings and sensations create an inner "cloud" which the rays of the sun – the intuition – cannot penetrate. These are intuitions from the Superconscious. We may spontaneously feel a sense of oneness with someone we have never met before; yet you know for sure that "this is my life companion." It may be the immediate certainty that you must leave your job and choose another career. Intuition is a powerful, unquestionable force of truth. Yet we may repress our intuition if the resistance from the Lower Unconscious is too strong.

Our consciousness may also reach to the intuitive dimension at the Supercon-scious level, where it may experience deep insights. In a meditation group that I led, several of us simultaneously experienced the solar system as a living organ-ism, evolving towards a defined goal. The planets were living beings with which we were deeply connected, and a large invisible hand led us towards our common goal. This experience was more real and intense than our usual physical reality. In all cases, we must train our will to let go of disturbing content and reject it when it enters the field of consciousness.

In the appendix there is an outline for a creative meditation aimed at developing intuition. In order to understand the truth about something, we must see it in its totality, in the context of the whole to which it belongs. We may ask: "What is the meaning of my life? ", "Why do I suffer? Only through intuition can we arrive at an answer to such questions. The meditation aims to create a channel linking three important points in our inner spiritual structure: a centre of being in the middle of the chest or "heart centre"; a "wisdom centre" in the brain, which is the head cen-tre; and the brilliant sphere of the soul above the head. This meditation strength-ens the connection between the self and the soul. This is the "elevator" Assagioli says we can use to reach the different floors of our inner house. Intuition lives in the terrace at the top of the Egg Diagram. Here we can see the stars and discover our intimate connection to the cosmos and the depths of Mother Earth.

The Superconscious houses an abundance of resources; through it we have access to a surplus of energy to motivate us in life. From it we receive the spiritual inspi-ration and aspiration to take the last step: the union of the self and the soul, the essential goal of transpersonal psychosynthesis, a journey we will take in the next chapter.

"There is no certainty; there is only adventure"

Roberto Assagioli

THE TRANSPERSONAL SELF
– THE WAY TO LOVE

The Transpersonal Self of each is in intimate union with the Transpersonal Self of all other individuals, however unconscious they may be of this. All Transpersonal Selves can be considered as "points" within the Universal Self. "
(Assagioli, 1974, p. 260)

The Transpersonal Self is the last of Assagioli's seven core concepts; it is also the most difficult to describe. Hidden beneath layers of thought, feeling and sensation it opens up to realities that transcend the intellect. Its character can best be described as light, energy and formless being.

Nevertheless, the ontological reality of the soul is fundamental to all training in Psychosynthesis. According to Assagioli we rarely experience the totality of the soul. We must start then with a theoretical understanding of its nature coupled with an experience of its guiding power. With this in mind let us begin with some perspectives on the direct experience of the soul.

In an interview Assagioli remarked that: "the first question I am generally asked is: What is psychosynthesis and in what ways does it differ from other therapies or conceptions of the human personality. First, it is based on experience; it is empirical and existential in the sense that it has grown out of my own experience and that of others. The description of the results is not a theory. It is a report of subjective experience. " (Besmer, 1973)

Assagioli did not write directly about his personal experiences; very little about himself can be found in his books. Yet after his death, notes he made while imprisoned during WWII were found in his archives, and in these he did write of his own experience. Assagioli was arrested because of his Jewish background and pacifist activities. An article by Schaub and Gulino (1994) reveals how Assagioli achieved a sense of inner freedom in prison. Although facing possible execution, he decided to turn his time in prison into a kind of spiritual retreat.

In his prison notes Assagioli wrote of experiencing "a sense of boundlessness, of no separation from all that is, a merging with the self of the whole." There was "first an outgoing movement, but not towards any particular object or individual- an overflowing or effusion in all directions, as the ways of an ever expanding sphere." Then came "a sense of universal love. Then the ability to focus the radiation (the universal love) towards some object or individual and at the same time to specialize its quality: a compassionate love towards the inmates of my prison and towards all prisoners and the inmates of hospitals, tender love to the members of my family; brotherly love towards my friends... " (Schaub, Gulino, 1994)

To understand what Assagioli means here we should recognize these aspects of the soul:

1. The soul in its static being and active radiation

2. The individual and universal nature of the soul

3. The masculine and feminine polarity of the soul

THE STATIC BEING AND ACTIVE RADIATION OF THE SOUL

In his prison notes Assagioli speaks of "a merging with the self of the whole" and an "overflowing or effusion in all directions." This seeming contradiction is rooted in two different but linked aspects of the soul, that of being and activity. The soul's character is like that of the self: a stable centre of pure consciousness and will. The difference is that when it merges with the universal Self, the soul's self-awareness is limitless. Here the experience of being is as a loving witness without limits, linked to the whole.

As Assagioli says, the soul continuously radiates higher states of consciousness, which we experience in the Superconscious. This is the radiation of universal love to our surroundings. The possibilities available here have their origin in the Transpersonal Self (1974, p. 119). Seen from this perspective, the experience of Superconscious energies is largely an experience of *the soul's emanations or radiations*. In other words, what we may experience as God, an angel or some paranormal phenomenon, are really – in some cases – our own emanations from a higher level of consciousness.

In his Talks on the Self (Undated 2) Assagioli explains the difference between the soul and its emanation:

"The Self radiates. Aristotle called it in that fine paradox the "Immovable mover." It is immovable but sets in motion everything else. I suggest that you meditate upon the immovable mover, and our centre the sun, that unknown mysterious entity that sends enormous radiation throughout our whole solar system and beyond. Also, a jewel is static, but sparkles. The jewel receives light and then reflects it and sends it back again, or even a simple mirror reflects most of the light it receives, so it is not so difficult to realize this paradox of the immovable mover."

Elsewhere he explains the difference between static being and activity:

"There is a basic difference between the flow of manifestation, the great working out of the cosmic plan, and the Transcendent. The Transcendent doesn't flow – the core, the inner jewel, the real centre-does not flow, it radiates." (Freund, 1983)

In an inspiring article based on notes from an interview with Assagioli, Jim Vargui writes that: "In this same way the Self is unchanging in essence, yet it sends out its energies, which are stepped down in intensity and transmitted through the Superconscious, and received, absorbed and utilized by the personality." (Assagioli, Undated 3)

It may seem relatively easy to comprehend the soul as radiating love and inspiration because we have an idea of these states in our own lives. Yet without direct experience, the idea of the soul's pure self-awareness may seem difficult to grasp. An insight that came to me while meditating may help.

In 2010 I led a meditation retreat, the aim of which was to observe consciousness in the present moment. After five hours of silence my mind seemed to fade into the background. I felt that the top of my head was somehow softening and i felt a sense of freedom and expansion. A kind of inner sky opened in my consciousness, which seemed to stretch into infinity. I sat at peace, simply "being."

I did not *see* this inner sky; it was me- a free, impersonal and limitless being. I could still think, but thinking felt like being in a straitjacket. In this expanded consciousness I felt a direct insight into my identity as a consciousness without physical form. My personal history and identity was seen against the backdrop of eternity. It was unquestionably irrelevant, yet somehow still important. There was a complete absence of personal sympathetic love; it was replaced by an oceanic sense of being love without an object. My sense of self was no longer restricted to the personal but was replaced with a certainty that we are all one consciousness. I had not become another, "I" was still "me". My sense of identity was the same but my identification was no longer tied to my personality. It was released into an open field of presence, which extended even beyond the Superconscious into the cosmic.

Moving from the self to the soul is like being on a plane that has cleared the clouds and entered bright, blue, open space. The difference is that the open sky we have entered is *ourselves*. Experiencing the soul in its static aspect as pure being is an experience of pure awareness. As Assagioli's says: "The Transpersonal Self is "outside" time and above it. It exists and lives in the dimension of the Eternal. " (1973)

So far our focus has been on the soul's static, emanating quality. We can call this the *open self* because it opens us to greater levels of unity with the world. In its most transcendent aspect it is universal, formless and non-manifest. It is a timeless consciousness, and is often referred to as the "the Ground of Being". This aspect of the soul can be found in Buddhism and Vedanta, and in the West it is associated with the Christian mystic Meister Eckhart.

THE INDIVIDUAL AND UNIVERSAL NATURE OF THE SOUL

The soul is not just open and boundless consciousness it also has an individual aspect. We awaken to this aspect through the Transpersonal Will-to-be-a-self. When we experience this polarity of the soul, we get a completely different sense of our essential being. On this point Assagioli quotes Father Auguste Gratry:

"I am fond of Auguste Gratry's description of contact with the Transpersonal Self because it is so vivid:

I felt as [if] it were an interior form ... full of strength, beauty and joy ... a form of light and flame, which sustained all my being: a steadfast, unchanging form, always the same, which I recovered again and again during the course of my life; yet I lost sight of it and forgot it at intervals, but always recognized it with joy and the exclamation: "Here is my real being"." (Miller, 1973)

Here we have an image of the soul as an unchanging inner form filled with strength, light and flame. Assagioli locates the soul both within and without the Egg Diagram in order to show its individuality and universality. From within the diagram the soul radiates its qualities. As Assagioli writes: "the Self radiates... downward to the personality, horizontally to other living beings, and vertically to the One Self."(Assagioli, Freund, 1983) Yet our individuality is never entirely lost even in the most universal states. As Lama Anagarika Govinda tells us:

"Individuality is not only the necessary and complementary opposite of universality, but the focal point through which alone universality can be experienced." (1974, p. 128)

Through the individual the unique becomes universal. Assagioli refers to the following quote of Radhakrishnan:

"The peculiar privilege of the human self is that he can consciously join and work for the whole and embody in his own life the purpose of the whole. . . . The two elements of selfhood: uniqueness (eachness), and universality (allness), grow together until at last the most unique becomes the most universal." (1974, p. 128)

We develop our individuality through our will and the choices we make. This means choosing that which we are rather than that which we are not. We develop our *unique selves* by using our will to pursue the purpose and qualities of life that reflect our true identity. There is never a moment in life without an underlying purpose or intention. The will is an energy we cannot escape, because we bring it to live whenever we make a choice.

Using an analogy from quantum physics we can say that the soul is both a particle and a wave. The will is our particle nature, and self-awareness is the wave. So Assagioli is right when he says that: "All Transpersonal Selves can be considered as "points" within the Universal Self." In meditation this will can be felt as an inner living force, a purposeful energy that *has a will to* something. It may be the soul's own Transpersonal Will to evolutionary enlightenment and service, or it may be God's will, the will of the universal Self. When Jesus' speaks of "my Father's will" he means this force.

Because the soul wants to transcend the limits of the personality and so be of service to the greater whole, "we need to face courageously and willingly the requirements for transcending the limitations of personal consciousness, without losing the centre of individual awareness. This is possible," Assagioli says: "because individuality and universality are not mutually exclusive; they can be united in a blissful synthetic realization. " (Assagioli, 1974, p. 113)

The soul also desires "communication with other selves" (1975, p. 87) as Assagioli describes in the opening quote of this chapter: *"The Transpersonal Self of each is in intimate union with the Transpersonal Self of all other individuals".* An exchange takes place between souls in the inner world, and for Assagioli the recognition of the group Self is a step towards the universal Self. (Undated 2)

THE SOUL'S FEMININE AND MASCULINE POLARITY.

Speaking to Sam Keen, Assagioli said that: "In the centre of the self is a union of the masculine and feminine, will and love, action and observation." (Keen, 1974)

Here Assagioli links the masculine to will and action and the feminine to love and observation (receptivity). The soul is thus dual, having a masculine and a feminine pole.

Our masculine and feminine polarity is itself static and active. We can see the masculine static form as divine fire and force. The static feminine form is universal openness, the experience of ourselves as a limitless and liberated loving witness.

The static masculine form is *purposeful*. We are unique individuals serving a specific purpose for the work of the universal Self. We are a point in the consciousness of the universal Self.

The soul's masculine will is like an inner force patiently pushing us past our comfort zones. It knows we are greater than we think we are, and it compels us to become authentically ourselves. This is the inner "king or "queen" who follows the call of the good, the true, and the beautiful. He accepts nothing less than the complete actualisation of what he can be. He extends the boundaries of what we thought was possible. It is clear that his is a will is to *action*.

The link between feminine love and observation requires deeper reflection. What does observation have in common with femininity and love? Both observation and love require openness. Observation in the sense we are using the word involves self-awareness and *receptivity* of the self – pure consciousness. So both love and observation *open* us so that we can identify with people, nature and the cosmos.

This openness expresses itself through our psychological functions. Physically we become relaxed and receptive. Emotionally we become sensitive to something other than ourselves. We speak of "open minds", when our thinking takes on a new perspective. Intuitively, we open to the divine. This openness includes our Ground of Being and identification with the whole. These are clearly feminine qualities.

The feminine aspect of the soul is expressed as the desire for belonging, unity and community. It opens hearts, and removes barriers separating us from others. The feminine part of the soul knows there is only the World Soul of which we all are an expression. From this perspective "Love your neighbour as yourself" means exactly that because your neighbour *is* yourself. Here we understand the soul as a way to greater love. The Transpersonal Will is the will to love, because God is love.

The universal soul is expressed though many individual "points of light". These vary in brightness, but the soul of humanity is one. Mystics have experienced this paradox and we can grasp it too intuitively, even if it is incomprehensible to the intellect. It represents the realization of our Buddha nature, or Christ-consciousness, what in Psychosynthesis we call Self-realization.

The masculine aspect of the soul seeks to perfect the purpose and development of the individual as a unique expression of the universal Self. The feminine part of soul connects the individual to the whole through identification with our humanity, nature and the world. It seeks to awaken the world to the unity of which it is an expression. By taking care of the cosmos it takes care of itself. Together the masculine and feminine polarity creates the good, the true, and the beautiful.

So far we have looked at a general anatomy of the soul. Many questions remain which can be answered only by awakening to our identity as soul. For now let us say that we are a "point of light within a greater light, which manifests itself through a physical body, with the aim of bringing love to the world."

Now let us take a look at how Assagioli understands the process of Self-realization.

THE PROCESS OF SELF-REALIZATION

Asked why our personal lives don't reflect the Superconscious, Assagioli replied:

"Because there are so many things in between. Between the personal self and the Higher Self there are all sorts of things – opaque, not transparent – that prevent the light, or refract it; all sorts of obstacles" (Freund, 1983)

With this in mind let's continue the soul's journey from body consciousness to nondual consciousness, exploring the obstacles along the way. As mentioned Assagioli's philosophy implies a notion of the soul's emanation. Here he talks about the symbol of resurrection: "It presupposes an emanastistic theory of the soul, descending , becoming one with matter, and then returning to its "home", the heavenly homeland-not as it was before, but enriched by the experience of self-awareness which has come to maturity in toil and conflict." (2007, p. 95)

In the Egg Diagram, the soul's descent to the self at the level of the personality is represented by the dotted line between the two levels of self-awareness. Assagioli writes: "Our spiritual being, the Self, which is the essential and most real part of us, is concealed, confined and "enveloped", first by the physical body with its sense

Enlightenment through the superconscious

impressions; then by multiplicity of the emotions and the different drives (fears, desires, attractions and repulsions); and finally by the restless activity of the mind. The liberation of the consciousness from the entanglements is an indispensable prelude to the revelation of the spiritual Centre." (1975, p. 214)

Self-realization means disidentifying with our given personality. It also means developing new qualities in our personality that reflects the soul's radiation. This is required in order to manifest the soul in the world. This means working with Ideal Models and subpersonalities.

Assagioli gives examples of two different ways to the soul which in practice must nevertheless be combined. The first involves anchoring superconscious states in the personality, via Ideal Models and symbols. The way involves purifying the personality and its reactions to these new states. This work gradually develops new qualities in the personality that enable us to better express the love and will of the soul. As mentioned we can call this enlightenment through the Superconscious, because it is an approach to the soul through an anchoring of superconscious qualities in the personality.

The second way is more direct. What does Assagioli mean by the direct awakening to the soul? "Self-realization, in this specific well-defined sense, means the momentary or more or less temporary identification or blending of the I-consciousness with the spiritual Self, in which the former, which is the reflection of the latter, becomes reunited, blended with the spiritual Self." (1975, p. 202) What has to be achieved is to expand the personal consciousness into the Self; "to reach up, following the thread or ray to the star". (Assagioli, 1975, p. 24)

Assagioli's "thread or ray" is the Bridge of Consciousness between the soul and the self (number 7 in the Egg Diagram in Chapter II). Assagioli speaks little about this, but it is nevertheless very important. The Bridge of Consciousness is our *direct* line of communication to the soul. The self is a projection of the soul and the Bridge of Consciousness must share its characteristics. It is a channel of pure self-awareness and will – a silent space – connecting the "earth and heavens".

This channel is formed of the male-female energy polarity discussed previously. I personally experience it as immovable wakefulness, this is the open feminine aspect. Then there is the dynamic force of will and *Life* itself. Basically there is only one will, the universal will, which is the force of evolution behind existence. Will and life are synonymous, and therefore one can agree that: "our Self (soul) is life and the personality is in the flow. The qualities of the personality should go with the flow, but not the Self. The great thing, difficult but possible, is to live at the same time in the eternal and in the temporal." (Assagioli, Freund, 1983)

For Assagioli life itself bring about synthesis at both biological and spiritual levels (1974, p. 32, 125, 130). The opening to the soul connects to a vital, potent, *fiery* being that *wants* something with our lives.

Assagioli sees this channel as "elastic" (Undated 2). It is "a channel of communication" (Assagioli, Freund, 1983), or, in another image, "an elevator" (Assagioli, Keen, 1974). We take it to "ascend" to the soul.

Let us look at how Assagioli can help us form an idea of the nature of this channel.

Writing in *Psychosynthesis* of the activation of the channel, Assagioli says: "The opening of the channel between the conscious and the superconscious levels, between the ego and the Self, and the flood of light, joy and energy which follows, often produce a wonderful release." (1975, p. 43) He also describes the gradual coming together of the self and the soul: "Before attaining reunification there is a time of dramatic "inner dialogue" – appeals, questions and answers-following by a gradual coming together and by ever more frequent and vivid sparks between the two poles as they approach one another until the point where they meet. They then separate again until that moment of great peace when the two become one." (2007, p. 78)

The soul's direct influence reaches the self through the Bridge of Consciousness. (Indirectly it passes through the Superconscious.) The self experiences the direct influence as a "calling" or a "pull". (See Chapter IX in *The Act of Will*.)

So how do we use this Bridge of Consciousness? Assagioli describes that it must be cleared before it becomes transparent to soul consciousness. There are, according to Assagioli, two primary methods we can apply to clear this channel. One is through the practice of disidentification and awareness meditation, which facilitates inner silence. The other is through the invocation of the soul asking for its intervention and then to wait for the soul's response.

Assagioli describes the effect of the silence: "After this must come the attainment and practice of "mental silence". This clears any obstacles between the mind and the higher cognitive functions, intuition, or enlightenment. More broadly it means purifying the channel between the personal "I" and the Transpersonal Self. This means purifying the whole personality and consciously withdrawing from identification with that personality though the cultivation of a divine "indifference" to its demands, so that one can then identify with the Self." (2007, p. 160)

Speaking with his students Assagioli instructed them in a meditation:

"But also with Self we can use each day for a moment, first a rapid recollection of the personal self, quieting as much as possible in a short time, relaxing the body, quieting the emotions, asking the mind to be so good as to keep still. And then in the measure we succeed in doing that, the elastic pull, the thread between the personal self and the Transpersonal Self can be considered as being elastic, and a good elastic. And when all the things which tie the personal self to the ordinary level are eliminated in a measure, the pull continuously operates and the personal self is drawn joyously upward toward the Self.

In the silence let us try, as much as possible, to go close to the Self, without strain or anxiety, but calmly, joyously and easily, helped by the central affirmation:

We are that Self, That Self are we.

Try to realize it in the silence." (Undated 2)

According to Assagioli it is a very radical process to achieve direct unity with the soul. Not only do we have to be disidentified from our personality, but also from the transpersonal states in the Superconscious. We can easily lose ourselves in ecstatic peak experiences and forget that the soul's purpose is to bring light to humanity. (Undated 2)

When we have disidentified from all states of consciousness, we awaken to the soul's static aspect : "In these cases there is a forgetfulness of all contents of consciousness, of all which forms the personality both on normal levels an those of the synthesized personality, which include superconscious or spiritual levels of life and experience; there is only the pure intense experience of the Self." (1975, p. 202) In order to strengthen the pure awareness of the observer, increasingly longer periods of mental silence is needed to create the inner void or sense of emptiness. This is why the communication channel is referred to as the "silent path".

In a conversation with one of his students Assagioli suggested the following technique to help with disidentification:

"There are some techniques which can help with disidentification. The first and most effective is the realization of infinity, eternity and universality. And that's completely scientific. The universe is practically infinite. The universe has no end and no beginning; perhaps, in millions and millions of years, but that's, for us, practically eternal. And then it's universal because all, everything, acts and reacts on everything. So, if you meditate, or just think, and try to realize this fact of infinity, eternity and universality, that will create an atmosphere of peace, of serenity." (Freund, 1983)

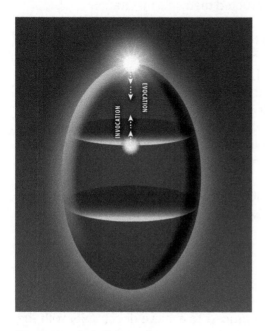

Illumination through invocation

In the same conversation with Diana Freund Assagioli describes the second method we can use to clear the channel, which is the personal self's invocation of the Transpersonal Self or soul.

"Invocation is the royal road. Invocation clears the channel. That thread between the personal self and the Transpersonal Self is really a channel, a channel of communication. And the most effective method is invocation."

"There are two chief ways for clearing that channel – one is to rise through techniques and discipline, upward. The personal self aspires and rises upward toward the Transpersonal Self and sometimes reaches the level of the Superconscious and then it can have peak experiences and broadening of consciousness and illumination. The other method is to attract the down pouring, what religious people call grace, but it isn't grace, it is scientific; it is an answer to an appeal. And that attracting can be done, perhaps even more effectively, when the personal self is in trouble. You know the saying-man's extremity, God's opportunity. Translated in scientific terms: In a psychological crisis the appeal of the personal self for help gives an opportunity for the Transpersonal Self to pour down its energy or its light or its love. You see that?"

Freund: Roberto interrupted himself to say that, of course, the two ways, coming from a harmonious condition or coming from one of anguish, were not actually separate. The channel they each cleared was the same, only the approach might be different. "Often the personal self tries to raise itself up to a certain point and succeeds, but it cannot go further – at that point, it invokes."

Roberto Assagioli continues the conversation with examples of specific invocations:

"May the light of the Self enlighten me".
"May the love of the Soul pervade me."
"May the peace of the Spirit enfold me."
(Freund, 1983)

THE THERAPEUTIC WORK WITH SOUL CONNECTION.

The best way to help our clients to clear the communication channel between the self and the soul is to instruct them in Awareness Based Meditation[13]. First they disidentify from the personality and become the observer. Next follows a sustained period with silence where they must use the will to let go of all distractions, and consciously choose to return to the silence. We can practice mental silence with or without invocation, but it is a useful technique to focus our attention.

The greatest challenge with this work is that the personality easily gets bored and impatient. Thoughts like: "nothing is happening " or "it's too uncomfortable to sit still" are not unusual. Let the client know that these thoughts represent our attachment to the personality. When we observe, accept and let go of these states we create a gradually expanding inner space.

Silence is saturated with soul quality. When the self is looking "up", the soul is looking "down", and this contact can be felt as silence. Some experience this silence as standing on the peak of the world's tallest mountain; others feel like they are lying on the bottom of the sea. Both are metaphors for the inexpressible; a quiet opening up to the great mystery.

It is sufficient to spend 15 minutes on these instructions. During this period, important impressions can be registered due to the effect of the silence; it is like the light from the sun or the moon reflecting on a perfectly *still sea*. These 15 minutes are not enough though to establish permanent contact with this inner silence. A daily practice and considerable more time is needed to develop the required sensitivity.

---

13 See Awareness Based Meditation in Appendix

The essence of Psychosynthesis is the union of love and will. The greatest art is the creation of a living synthesis in our hearts. We are here to demonstrate that we are points of light within a greater light, and our purpose is to bring love to life on earth.

Let us end this chapter- and the book- with an instruction from Assagioli who is beautifully illustrating how disidentification is replaced with the identification with the soul.

"In the night-darkened room, with only our globe of the universe lit, both of us sat, eyes lowered, bodies relaxed and comfortable, to meditate, Roberto began, speaking slowly: "More radiant than the sun. (RA: I comment on that: that means that the spiritual radiance, the radiance of the higher plane is greater than the enormous radiance of the physical sun. Do you realize what that means, more radiant than the sun?)

"Purer than the snow. (That means completely disidentified with all lower contents. The Self is disidentified from the purest things we can conceive, like the snow.)

"And subtler than the ether (because a being in that high plane, the vibrations, are thinner and more powerful) is the Self, the spirit within us. (But we are in spirit, and in truth, and so we are from eternity.) I am that Self, that Self am I. (Only realizing the Self, for each of us, is part of the one Universal Self, because at that level there are no separations, no loneliness, no distances.)

"Now you realize better the meaning of this. So let us meditate on it and realize…" Very slowly he intoned,

"More Radiant than the sun
Purer than the snow
Subtler than the ether
Is the Self, the Spirit within us. We are that Self
That Self are we."

(Freund, 1983)

"You are here with all your past. I am here with all my past. And then we'll proceed into our futures. But our souls, our Selves, there we are one"

Roberto Assagioli

APPENDIX

- Roberto Assagioli – a short Biography

- Training – a statement by Roberto Assagioli

- Assagioli's Disidentification Exercise

- Awareness Based Meditation

- Creative Meditation on the Ideal Model

- The SoulFlow Method

- Creative Meditation on Intuitive Impressions

- References

BY KENNETH SØRENSEN

ROBERTO ASSAGIOLI
– His Life and Work

Roberto Assagioli was very reluctant to give interviews about his life, as he thought that it was wrong to focus on him as a person. Focus had to be on Psychosynthesis. However, pushed by his colleagues he agreed at the end of his life to have a biography made, and he chose the Boston psychotherapist Eugine Smith to make it. Assagioli died shortly afterwards, in 1974, and the biography was never made. So what we know from Assagioli's personal life, we know from his own publications and from people who have worked with him, or who in other ways have had knowledge of him.

Assagioli's childhood and youth

Roberto Marco Grego was born in Venice, Italy, February 27, 1888. Here he spent his childhood. Roberto's father died when Roberto was 2 years old, and his mother, Elana Kaula (1863-1925) remarried Dr. Alessandro Emanuele Assagioli in 1891, which gave Roberto his last name.

Assagioli grew up in a cultural upper-middle-class Jewish family with an interest in art, music and literature, where he received private lessons, as was typical for his time and class. His appreciation of beauty, art and music was stimulated early, and is clearly seen as a part of the basis for Psychosynthesis.

It may have been his mother's studies of Theosophy which early in his life awoke his great interest in Eastern philosophies and in the higher spiritual potentials of mankind. Theosophy is a philosophy which was formulated in the late 19th century, and which developed into a movement with its roots in North America, later spreading to Europe and the East. The philosophy is even older, with roots in the mystic traditions of both East and West.

In his home Italian, English and French were spoken. He was a curious child, eager to learn, and later he learned to speak Greek, Latin, German, Russian and Sanskrit before he was 18 years of age. He loved to formulate himself in writing, and already at the age of fifteen he published the article "Unconscious Wishes and Conscious Work" in the periodical *Giornale de Venezia*.

Roberto Assagioli   *Assagioli with family*

At an early age he was interested in international relations and he travelled a lot, also alone. At the age of 17 he went to Russia, and this promoted his ideals of liberty, created through non-violence and non-dogmatic social systems. His many journeys taught him that man is the same, no matter which country he may come from, and that deep down in everybody is a desire to develop one's highest potential.

In 1904 his parents moved to Florence where he lived most of his life. Here he studied at the faculty of medicine, Istitution di Studi Superiori, and received his medical degree, specializing in neurology and psychiatry.

After World War I he lived and worked for some years in Rome, where he married Nella in 1922 (see picture). They had a son the same year, who was named Ilario Assagioli. The marriage was close and loving and lasted for 50 years.

Education and first articles

In 1907 he began a doctoral dissertation and finished it at the age of 21. Here he also presented a vision of a holistic approach to psychology with a focus on human growth and human experiences with spiritual dimensions. This approach aimed at living a more complete life, and as he himself puts it, "To live as well as possible, and look at oneself with a smile."

Almost at the same time he finished a critical article on psychoanalysis, which he considered limited and unfinished. However, he was deeply involved in the exploration and development of Freud's discoveries concerning childhood and the unconscious. In an interview by Sam Keen from *Psychology Today*, December 1974, Assagioli answers the question about the major differences between psychoanalysis and Psychosynthesis:

"We pay far more attention to the higher unconscious and to the development of the transpersonal self. In one of his letters Freud said, "I am interested only in the basement of the human being." Psychosynthesis is interested in the whole building. We try to build an elevator which will allow a person access to every level of his personality. After all, a building with only a basement is very limited. We want to open up the terrace where you can sunbathe or look at the stars." (Keen, 1974)

His main criticism was that psychoanalysis was too focussed on the pathological side of the psyche, and failed to focus on and strengthen what is healthy, as a path to healing. Also, Assagioli said that human consciousness held more layers of consciousness than Freud's model included. He wanted to create a psychology which contained the urges, but also love, will, wisdom and spirituality. In other words, a psychology with a focus on the entire human being.

In the same period he wrote his treatise he had his psychiatric practise at San Salvis psychiatric Hospital.

In 1909 he published his new ideas in the periodical *La Psicologia delle idée-forze e la Psicagogia*. At that time the academic world was very reluctant to accept Assagioli's hypotheses.

Already in the beginning of the 20th century he published several articles, bordering on medicine, pedagogy, philosophy, culture and religion, which later formed the basis of Psychosynthesis. In 1906 he published his first comprehensive article on Psychosynthesis in Farrari's magazine, inspired by Freud's article *Jokes and their relation to the unconscious*, entitled *Gli effete del riso el le loro applicazioni pedagoiche*. It dealt with the significance of laughter and its relation to education. The article is known today under the title "Smiling Wisdom". (Assagioli, Undated 8)

Assagioli had a broad interest in philosophy and culture and participated in groups of young liberal free thinkers in the Florence of that time. He was one of the most active editors of the cultural magazine "Leonardo" in Florence up to 1907.

The Editors of Leonardo: Assagioli, Papini og Vailati

The magazine was the meeting place for the young intellectuals of Florence. It was founded in 1903 by one of his closest friends, self-educated author and intellectual Giovanni Papini.

At an early stage Assagioli had a clear feeling that the human being was not just a high-ranking animal or a machine. This was in opposition to the ruling concept, namely that medicine and psychology could be understood in the same way as other technical fields.

In 1911 he began formulating the concepts of Psychosynthesis, and he continued to dedicate his entire professional life to this task.

Psychiatric career and development of Psychosynthesis

Having finished his studies in 1910 Assagioli was trained in psychiatry in Switzerland with Eugen Bleuler in the psychiatric hospital Burghölzli in Zürich. Bleuler was the pioneer who defined schizophrenia, and he was one of the first doctors to accept psychoanalysis. At the time Assagioli opened the first psychoanalytic practice in Italy. It is said that he was not satisfied, neither with his work nor the results of his clinical work. Alongside with his studies at Bleuler's he continued to

Roberto Assagioli

develop his psychology in Italy. At first he called it Bio-Psychosynthesis, and later Psychosynthesis. He was not the first to use the term, psychosynthesis, it was also used by Bezzola, Jung and others.

In his early clinical practice Assagioli applied psychoanalytic techniques, but his vision of the human being urged him to compose a large coherent apparatus of analysis to include love, wisdom, creativity and will. His attitude was not that psychoanalysis was wrong, but rather that it was incomplete.

Already while working in Zürich, he was absorbed in psychological studies with a special interest in the works of William James and Henri Bergson. Here he met with Carl Gustav Jung and befriended him. According to Assagioli himself, it was Jung's psychology which was closest to Psychosynthesis. (Assagioli, 1967b)

As the only Italian, Assagioli was a member of the Freud Society of Zürich, which consisted of pioneers of psychoanalysis. He was also a member of The International Psychoanalytic Society. He was deeply involved in the exploration of psychoanalysis, and with Freud and Jung he contributed to the foreword of the official *Jahrbuch für Psychoanalytische und Psychopathologische Forschungen*, in which he wrote an article, entitled "Freud's Theories in Italy". He contributed articles and commentaries to Freud's second periodical *Psychoanalysis*. He started a study group with 19 members with the purpose of understanding the human psyche.

A published letter from Jung to Freud shows Assagioli's hopes of bringing psychoanalysis to Italy:

"A very pleasant and perhaps valuable acquaintance, our first Italian, a Dr. Assagioli from the psychiatric clinic in Florence. Prof. Tanzi assigned him our work for a dissertation. The young man is very intelligent, seems to be extremely knowledgeable and is an enthusiastic follower, who is entering the new territory with the proper brio. He wants to visit us next spring." (Roberto Assagioli 1888-1988, published by the Italian Psychosynthesis Institute)

Assagioli never met with Freud in person, but corresponded with him.

In the history of psychoanalysis he is one of the first Italian pioneers. That in itself made him stand out in a time where all studies of the human mind were considered with scepticism. Simultaneously he worked – as we have seen – to develop Psychosynthesis. He had his ideas and thoughts communicated among other places in his periodical *Psiche* during 1912-1915, where it had to close because of the war. His articles were later published in another periodical, named *Ultra*. They are said to have had an explosive effect on the culture of the time. In *Psiche* he translated and published the first of Freud's writings in the Italian language, authorized by Freud himself.

During World War I he served as a doctor and a psychiatrist.

The Development of Psychosynthesis

In 1926 Assagioli opened the first institute in Rome, Istituto di Cultura e Terapia Psichica, which later became Istituto de Psicosintesi. In the letter of invitation to the opening it is said that his inauguration speech will be about how to develop the will. One of his most important books later got the title *The Act of Will*. It appeared shortly before his death in 1974. In 1927 the Institute published a book called *A New Method of Treatment – Psychosynthesis*. And in 1933 he was allowed to call his school in Florence Istituto de Psicisintesi. The institute was headed by Lady Spalletti Raspoini, who was also the president of "The National Council of Italian Women".

In 1928 he gives a series of lectures at the institute, called *The Energies Latent in Us and Their Use in Education and in Medicine*, which in time come to shape the theoretical basis for the work with opposites. In short, Psychosynthesis works with the hypothesis that any emotion or reaction has an opposite, and the task is to unite and create a synthesis between the two. What brings about the synthesis is the active I, the observer, the controlling factor in the human being, and later the higher Self.

Assagioli agreed with Freud that healing childhood traumas and the development of a healthy ego were necessary goals. But in broad outline his work tried to show that human development does not stop there, and that the healthy person has a potential for growth, which Maslow later gave the name "self-actualization". Assagioli went further and tried to show that human potential also holds a possibility of experiences with spiritual and transpersonal dimensions.

Thus Psychosynthesis is the earliest forerunner of the humanistic and transper-

Assagioli in army service

sonal psychology of the 1960's which forms the third and fourth wave in the history of Western psychology.

Upon this basis he becomes the co-editor of both *Journal of Humanistic Psychology* and *Journal of Transpersonal Psychology*.

It was important to Assagioli that Psychosynthesis be viewed as an open psychological system in continuous development, rather than a religious or philosophical doctrine. In his first book *Psychosynthesis*, he writes:

"Psychosynthesis does not aim nor attempt to give a metaphysical or a theological explanation of the great Mystery – it leads to the door, but stops there." (p.5)

Therefore it was also important for him that the various schools and institutes, which arose around the USA and in Europe, were independent and not controlled centrally. He was not at all interested in leading any kind of movement or organisation, and he refused to have any administrative control over the development of Psychosynthesis.

Assagioli's fundamental view includes both the individual and society, with a focus on synthesis and unification rather than analysis and splitting into smaller parts. Assagioli attempts to create a psychology with synthesis between Eastern mysticism and philosophy, and Western psychoanalysis and logic. It was important to Assagioli that Psychosynthesis remained scientific.

Assagioli's inspirations

Like C. G. Jung, Assagioli was inspired by Eastern and Western mysticism and esotericism. As mentioned before, both his mother and his wife were theosophists. And the source of Theosophy from the Hindu/Neo-Platonic tradition is essential in his thinking. The coherence with Eastern and Western mystic traditions is clear in his concept of the Self, which highly resembles the Eastern description of "Atman".

To Assagioli the Self is a nucleus of consciousness and will, which is not synony-mous with the body, the emotions or the thoughts. Self-realisation to Assagioli is an evolution of consciousness, where still higher expansions of consciousness lead to a unification with the universal Self. These thoughts are also characteristic of Eastern yoga-traditions. The neo-Platonic element shows in his concept of em-anation. In his book *Transpersonal Development* p. 102 he writes:

"We have now reached the fifteenth group of symbols, that of resurrection and return, what in the gospels is referred to as the return of the prodigal son to his fa-ther's house. This is a return to a previous state and points to a return to the original primordial being. This presupposes an emanatistic theory of the soul, descending, becoming one with matter, and then returning to its "home", the heavenly home-land –not as it was before, but enriched by the experience of self-awareness which has come to maturity in toil and conflict"

Roberto Assagioli with Alice Bailey and friends

Assagioli also has several references to Western mystics, like John of the Cross and Saint Francis of Assisi. Within Western psychology there is no doubt that William James, C. G. Jung and Viktor Frankl were spiritually related fellows. All his life, in his understanding of the pathological conditions in the lower unconscious, he drew on many of the psychodynamic theories. He believed that prior to spiritual development there had to be a psychoanalysis – not in the classic sense of the word – but a deep psychological transformation.

But to establish his true spiritual affiliations, Theosophy is the stronger candidate. He was a close friend of esoterist Alice Bailey and joined her Arcane School by the beginning of the 30's. He also wrote the foreword to the Italian edition of Alice Bailey's commentary to Patanjali's Yoga Sutras.

He did not want publicity about this, because he wanted to be seen as a scientist, first and foremost. When psychologist Jim Fadiman visited Assagioli in 1972, he noticed a portrait of Madame Blavatsky, the founder of Theosophy, in his waiting room. Answering the question, why it was necessary to be silent about his esoteric affiliations Assagioli said, "It is my religion, and until I die I want silence about it." (Schuller, 1988)

He never tried to hide that his religion also included reincarnation. In an interview with Sam Keen he relates:

"Death looks to me primarily like a vacation. There are many hypotheses about death and the idea of reincarnation seems the most sensible to me. I have no direct knowledge about reincarnation but my belief puts me in good company with hundreds of millions of Eastern people, with the Buddha and many others in the West."

But Assagioli clearly distinguished between his own religion and his work as a transpersonal psychologist and psychiatrist. He was not an intellectual in the normal sense of the word, he was far more a mystic, and his theories about man were to a very high degree based on his own inner experience

Important Developments

In the 1930's he published several articles, later to appear in his first book: *Psychosynthesis* in 1965. It is here we find two of the most important articles on psychosynthesis "Dynamic Psychology and Psychosynthesis and Self-realization and Psychological Disturbances". In the first article from 1933 he presented for the first time his oval diagram, or as it is also called, the "egg-diagram", as a picture of the human psyche, where the relationship between the conscious, the unconscious, and the collective unconscious is outlined, establishing the phases of psychosynthesis. The second article is about crises connected to spiritual development.

In 1938 the Instituto de Psicosintesi in Florence was shut down by Mussolini's Fascist government, being critical of Assagioli's Jewish background, his humanism and internationalism. That same year he was arrested, imprisoned and put into solitary confinement for a month. This turned out to be of great importance to the further development of Psychosynthesis. He is said to have told his friends that his time in prison was an interesting and valuable experience, which gave him the possibility to exercise psycho-spiritual practice. Feeling powerless, he made an important discovery about the will. He discovered that he himself could choose how to react to his imprisonment.

So he changed the imprisonment into an opportunity to investigate the inner areas of consciousness by meditating several hours daily, and writing articles on his experiences. Later he related that he had never before felt such peace, and enjoyed so much being alive. Just before his death he worked on an article about this experience, entitled *Freedom in Prison*.

World War II was a hard time for his family, as Assagioli lived underground and often had to sleep under the stars. In 1943 he was actually hunted and had to hide in distant mountains. Here he met with a British parachute-soldier and several escaped prisoners. He experienced two dangerous episodes where Nazis chased him personally. They plundered and destroyed his family's farm near Florence.

This life during the war probably had a part in weakening the health of both himself and his son, Ilarios, who died from a severe lung disease at the young age of 28.

After the end of the war in 1945, Assagioli was able to resume spreading and developing Psychosynthesis. The Institute de Psicosintesi was re-established in Florence, where it functions to-day. In 1951 he established The Italian Union for Progressive Judaism, a branch of The World Judaism Union for Progressive Judaism, based on the concept of openness, understanding and cooperation between peoples and religions with the purpose of creating an organic and creative synthesis of the entire humanity.

Psychosynthesis began spreading to the USA and Europe after World War II. In 1957 The Psychosynthesis Research Foundation was established in Delaware, USA. It was later transferred to New York, and this foundation published several of Assagioli's texts in English. In 1958, following Assagioli's visit there, a school was established in Valmy, USA, occupied with the education and research of Psychosynthesis. Later other schools of Psychosynthesis were established many places in the USA, Switzerland, Austria and Great Britain. In those years Assagioli cooperated with A. Maslow, whose article *The Creative Attitude* was published by The Psychosynthesis Research Foundation.

Roberto Assagioli

During the 1970's and 80's Psychosynthesis expanded in North America and Europe. Many schools appeared, of which many later have been closed. Today it is possible to take an MA in Psychosynthesis from the two institutes in London.

In Scandinavia there are institutes for Psychosynthesis in Sweden, Norway, Finland and in Denmark preparations are being made for an institute.

Today Psychosynthesis is recognized in The European Association for Psychotherapies (EAP) with its own umbrella organization The European Federation for Psychosynthesis Psychotherapists.

During his career Assagioli wrote several hundred articles and essays, of which many have been translated into several languages. A great number of these can be found on www.psykosyntese.dk. The best known books are *Psychosynthesis* from 1965, and *The Act of Will* from 1974. Even up to his death he worked on a book, which was published posthumously, entitled *Transpersonal Development*. Another small book exists from his hand, *Psychosynthesis Typology*, which unfolds a sketch of the seven ways to self-realisation.

Piero Ferrucci about Assagioli

We will finish this biographical description of the life and works of Assagioli with a statement from Piero Ferrucci, one of the students of Assagioli, and himself a prominent teacher and author. Due to his cooperation with Assagioli through many years, he is probably one of the persons, who knew Assagioli best. Among other books he is the author of *What We May Be* and *Inevitable Grace*. In his foreword to *A Psychology with a Soul* by Jean Hardy, Piero Ferrucci writes:

"As far as I know, Roberto Assagioli is the only individual who has participated personally and actively in the unfurling of two distinct and fundamental revolutions in twentieth century psychology.

The first revolution was the birth of psychoanalysis and depth psychology in the beginning of the century: Assagioli, then a young medical student, presented his MD dissertation on psychoanalysis, wrote in the official Jahrbuch side by side with Freud and Jung, and was part of the Zurich Freud Society, the group of early psychoanalytical pioneers. The idea of unconscious processes in the mind made a lasting impression on him, an impression which he later developed into a variety of hypotheses well beyond the boundaries of orthodox psychoanalysis.

The second revolution in which Assagioli participated was the creation of humanistic and transpersonal psychology in the 1960's. A. H. Maslow was the pioneer of these new developments. The main idea was simple: rather than focusing on pathology in order to define the human being (as psychoanalysis had all too often done), or on the structural similarities between the human and the animal nervous system (as behaviourism suggested), the humanistic and transpersonal point of view, while not denying the findings of the other schools, put the main emphasis on the organism's striving for wholeness, on the human being's potential for growth, expansion of consciousness, health, love and joy.

Richness in contacts and interchanges was quite important in Assagioli's background: consider such diverse acquaintances (some of them brief, others lasting) as Italian idealist Benedetto Croce, Russian esotericist P. D. Ouspensky, German philosopher Hermann Keyserling, Indian poet Rabindranath Tagore, Sufi mystic Inhayat Khan, Zen Scholar D. T. Suzuki, Tibet's explorer Alexandra David Neel, plus psychologists Viktor Frankl, the founder of logotherapy, Robert Desoille, creator of the guided daydream, and C. G. Jung himself, before and after his break with psychoanalysis. Such contacts, coupled with a life of experimentation and reflection, provided an undoubtedly wide perspective for Assagioli's creation, which he called Psychosynthesis."

REFERENCES:

- Assagioli, Roberto, *Life As a Game And Stage Performance*. Psychosynthesis Training Center, 1983.

- Ferrucci et. al, *Roberto Assagioli 1888-1988*, Instituto di Psiconsintesi, 1988

- Firman, John, *Dimension of Growth* http://www.psykosyntese.dk/a-129/

- Firman, John, *A psychology of the Spirit*, Suny, 2002

- Hardy, Jean, *A Psychology With a Soul*, Woodgrange Press, 1996

- Keen, Sam, *The Golden Mean of Roberto Assagioli*, Psychology Today, December 1974, http://www.psykosyntese.dk/a-103/

- Löfwendahl, Peter, *Upptäck Psykosyntesen*, Huma Nova Förlag, 2003.

- Russell, Douglas, *Psychosynthesis and Western Psychology* http://www.psykosyntese.dk/a-69/

- Schuller, Michael, *Psychosynthesis in North America*, 1988 published by the author

- Unknown, *In Memoriam: Roberto Assagioli (1888-1974),* Synthesis Journal II,1975

- *The Life and Work of Roberto Assagioli*, Sunypress.edu (author unknown)

TRAINING
– A statement by Roberto Assagioli

1. Undertaking training in psychosynthesis means beginning to learn about psychosynthesis and experiment with it on oneself, in order then to help others to use it on themselves. Before being able to communicate psychosynthesis to others, we must have experimented with it in depth on ourselves. Intellectual knowledge is not sufficient. Every single technique must be tried out at length on oneself. Only thus shall we be in a position to communicate it with authority.

2. While psychosynthesis is offered as a synthesis of various therapies and educational approaches, it is well to keep in mind that it possesses its own original and central essence. This is so as not to present a watered-down and distorted version, or one over-coloured by the concepts and tendencies of the various contemporary schools. Certain fundamental facts exist, and their relative conceptual elaboration, deep experience and understanding are central, and constitute the sine qua non of psychosynthetic training. These experiences are:

   - Disidentification

   - The personal self

   - The will: good, strong, skilful

   - The Ideal Model

   - Synthesis (in its various aspects)

   - The superconscious

   - The Transpersonal Self (it is not possible in the majority of cases to have a complete experience of this; but it is good to have some theoretical knowledge of its characteristics and the experience of its guidance).

3. Different levels of meaning are associated with each of these experiences,

none of which will ever be definite and complete. Continuance of one's training, however, will always reveal new and more interesting aspects, which link the experiences together. That is to say, each experience will be seen to be not isolated, but to imply others. It is therefore unrealistic to speak in terms of "having understood or not having understood". Understanding being ever partial, belief in having understood all indicates lack of understanding. It is a question of a gradual process.

4. The preceding point clearly suggests that the best attitude to adopt – and one that is at the same time more realistic, more honest and more effective in achieving rapid progress in training – is one compounded of humility, patience and experimentation.

5. Psychosynthesis is not identified with any technique or practice. Despite the fact that in group work use is often made of guided imagination and visualization exercises, psychosynthesis can by no means be levelled down to these techniques.

6. One can know all the principal ones and still not have grasped the spirit of psychosynthesis, and vice versa. Real training entails both these factors – intuitive understanding of the spirit of psychosynthesis and a sound technical knowledge.

Psychosynthesis functions in five main fields: the t*herapeutic* (psychotherapy; doctor-patient relations); *personal integration and actualization* (realization of one's own potentialities); *the educational* (psychosynthesis by parents and by educators in school of all degrees); the *interpersonal* (marriage, couples etc.); *the social* (right social relations within groups and between groups).

Each one can choose a particular field of work and specialize in it alone. Being familiar with the other fields, however, is valuable, since all fields are interconnected. But the field of self-actualization and integration being the heart of psychosynthesis, a thorough knowledge of it is necessary for anyone operating in the other fields.

7. The achievement of a certain degree of mental polarization is required for becoming a psychosynthesist. This does not mean developing the mind while repressing or ignoring the emotions. On the contrary it means cultivating the mind and not only the emotions, as well as acquiring a personal centre of gravity within a sort of balanced and loving "reasonableness" (in the widest and deepest sense of the word) rather than an uncontrolled emotionalism.

8. Training in psychosynthesis has no end. At a certain point hetero-training (meaning training guided by someone else) is replaced by self-training. Psychosynthetic self-training should never stop. Psychosynthesis is an open system: there is no end to it, but only temporary halting places.

9. Only when one has acquired a thorough training (and this in the judgement of whoever is directing the training) is it wise to commence to engage in psychosynthesis professionally with individuals or groups. The time this needs is impossible to establish in advance, there being many variables involved.

10. Since the training is endless, it is wise to modify both the duration and intensity of the hetero-training received: by intensity is meant the number of sessions a month.

11. Since each can only be a partial expression of what we call "psychosynthesis", it is well to gain experience of psychosynthesis through the methods and personalities of various psychosynthesists.

12. Like any other form of training, training in psychosynthesis can fall away and become distorted after a certain period of time, particularly when not actively maintained and continued. Therefore it pays to undergo a refresher period now and then.

BY ROBERTO ASSAGIOLI

SELF-IDENTIFICATION EXERCISE
– Disidentification and Self-Identification

We are dominated by everything with which our self becomes identified. We can dominate, direct, and utilize everything from which we disidentify ourselves.

The central, fundamental experience of self-consciousness, the discovery of the "I," is implicit in our human consciousness.[14] It is that which distinguishes our consciousness from that of the animals, which are conscious but not self-conscious. But generally this self-consciousness is indeed "implicit" rather than explicit. It is experienced in a nebulous and distorted way because it is usually mixed with and veiled by the *contents* of consciousness.

This constant input of influences veils the clarity of consciousness and produces, spurious identifications of the self with the content of consciousness, rather than with consciousness *itself*. If we are to make self-consciousness explicit, clear, and vivid, we must first disidentify ourselves from the contents of our consciousness.

More specifically, the habitual state for most of us is to be identified with that which seems, at any one time, to give us the greatest sense of aliveness, which seems to us to be most real, or most intense.

This identification with a part of ourselves is usually related to the predominant function or focus of our awareness, to the predominant role we play in life. It can take many forms. Some people are identified with their bodies. They experience themselves, and often talk about themselves, mainly in terms of sensation; In other words they function as if they *were* their bodies. Others are identified with their feelings; they experience and describe their state of being in affective terms, and believe their feelings to be the central and most intimate part of themselves, while thoughts and sensations are perceived as more distant, perhaps somewhat separate. Those who are identified with their minds are likely

---

14 "Self-consciousness" is used here in the purely psychological sense of being aware of oneself as a distinct individual and not in the customary sense of egocentric and even neurotic "self-centeredness."

to describe themselves with intellectual constructs, even when asked how they *feel*. They often consider feelings and sensations as peripheral, or are largely unaware of them. Many are identified with a role, and live, function, and experience themselves *in terms of that role*, such as "mother," "husband," "wife," "student," "businessman," "teacher," etc.

This identification with only *a part* of our personality may be temporarily satisfactory, but it has serious drawbacks. It prevents us from realizing the experience of the "I," the deep sense of self-identification, of knowing who we are. It excludes, or greatly decreases, the ability to identify with all the other parts of our personality, to enjoy them and utilize them to their full extent. Thus our "normal" expression in the world is limited at any one time to only a fraction of what it can be.

The conscious—or even unconscious—realization that we somehow do not have access to much that is in us can cause frustration and painful feelings of inadequacy and failure.

Finally, a continuing identification with either a role or a predominant function leads often, and almost inevitably, to a precarious life situation resulting sooner or later in a sense of loss, even despair, such as in the case of an athlete who grows old and loses his physical strength; an actress whose physical beauty is fading; a mother whose children have grown up and left her; or a student who has to leave school and face a new set of responsibilities. Such situations can produce serious and often very painful crises. They can be considered as more or less partial psychological "deaths." No frantic clinging to the waning old "identity" can avail. The true solution can be only a "rebirth," that is, entering into a new and broader identification. This sometimes involves the whole personality and requires and leads to an awakening or "birth" into a new and higher state of *being*. The process of death and rebirth was symbolically enacted in various mystery rites and has been lived and described in religious terms by many mystics. At present it is being rediscovered in terms of transpersonal experiences and realizations.

This process often occurs without a clear understanding of its meaning and often against the wish and will of the individual involved in it. But a conscious, purposeful, willing cooperation can greatly facilitate, foster, and hasten it.

It can be best done by a deliberate exercise of *disidentification* and *self-identification*. Through it we gain the *freedom* and the power of choice to be identified with, or disidentified from, any aspect of our personality, according to what seems to us most appropriate in each situation. Thus we can learn to master, direct, and utilize all the elements and aspects of our personality, in an inclusive and harmonious synthesis. Therefore this exercise is considered as basic in psychosynthesis.

IDENTIFICATION EXERCISE

This exercise is intended as a tool for achieving the Consciousness of the self, and the ability to focus our attention sequentially on each of our main personality aspects, roles, etc. We then become clearly aware of and can examine their qualities while maintaining the point of view of the observer and recognizing that *the observer is not that which he observes.*

In the form which follows, the first phase of the exercise— the disidentification— consists of three parts dealing with the physical, emotional, and mental aspects of awareness. This leads to the self-identification phase. Once some experience is gained with it, the exercise can be expanded or modified according to need, as will be indicated further on.

Procedure

Put your body in a comfortable and relaxed position, and slowly take a few deep breaths (preliminary exercises of relaxation can be useful). Then make the following affirmation, slowly and thoughtfully:

"I *have* a body but I *am not* my body. My body may find itself in different conditions of health or sickness, it may be rested or tired, but that has nothing to do with my-*self,* my real 'I.' I value my body as my precious instrument of experience and of action in the outer world, but it is *only an instrument.* I treat it well, I seek to keep it in good health, but it is not myself. I *have* a body, but I *am not* my body."

Now close your eyes, recall briefly in your consciousness the general substance of this affirmation, and then gradually focus your attention on the central concept: "I *have* a body but I *am not* my body." Attempt, as much as you can, to realize this as an experienced fact in your consciousness. Then open your eyes and proceed the same way with the next two stages:

"I *have* emotions, but I *am not* my emotions. My emotions are diversified, changing, and sometimes contradictory. They may swing from love to hatred, from calm to anger, from joy to sorrow, and yet my essence—my true nature—does not change. 'I' remain. Though a wave of anger may temporarily submerge me, I know that it will pass in time; Therefore I *am not* this anger. Since I can observe and understand my emotions, and then gradually learn to direct, utilize, and integrate them harmoniously, it is clear that they are not my *self.* I have emotions, but I am not my emotions.

"*I have* a mind but I *am not* my mind. My mind is a valuable tool of discovery and expression, but *it is not* the essence of my being. Its contents are constantly changing as it embraces new ideas, knowledge, and experience. Often it refuses to obey me! Therefore, it cannot be me my self. It is *an organ of knowledge* in regard to both the outer and the inner worlds, but it is not my self. I have a mind, but I am not my mind."

Next comes the phase of *identification*. Affirm slowly and thoughtfully:

"After the disidentification of *myself*, the 'I,' from the contents of consciousness, such as sensations, emotions, thoughts, *I recognize and affirm that I am a center of pure self-consciousness*. I am a *center of will*, capable of observing, directing, and using all my psychological processes and my physical body."

Focus your attention on the central realization: "*I am a center of pure self-consciousness and of will.*" Attempt, as much as you can, to realize this as an *experienced* fact in your awareness.

As the purpose of the exercise is to achieve a specific state of consciousness, once that purpose is grasped much of the procedural detail can be dispensed with. Thus, after having" practiced it for some time—and some might do this from the very beginning—one can modify the exercise by going swiftly and dynamically through each of the stages of disidentification, using only the central affirmation of each stage and concentrating on its *experiential* realization.

I *have* a body, but I *am not* my body.

I *have* emotions, but I *am not* my emotions.

I *have* a mind, but I *am not* my mind.

At this point it is valuable to make a deeper consideration of the stage of self-identification along the following lines:

"What am I then? What remains after having disidentified me from my body, my sensations, my feelings my desires, my mind, my actions? It is the essence of myself—a center of pure self-consciousness. It is the permanent factor in the ever varying flow of my personal life. It is that which gives me a sense of being, of permanence, of inner balance. I affirm my identity with this center and realize its permanency and its energy, (pause).

"I recognize and affirm myself as a center of pure self-awareness and of creative, dynamic energy. I realize that from this center of true identity I can learn to observe, direct, and harmonize all the psychological processes and the physical body. I will to achieve a constant awareness of this fact in the midst of my everyday life, and to use it to help me and give increasing meaning and direction to my life."

As the attention is shifted increasingly to the *state of consciousness,* the identification stage also can be abridged. The goal is to gain enough facility with the exercise so that one can go through each stage of disidentification swiftly and dynamically in a short time, and then remain in the "I" consciousness for as long as desired. One can then—*at will,* and at any moment— disidentify from any overpowering emotion, annoying thought, inappropriate role, etc., and from the vantage point of the detached observer gain a clearer understanding of the situation, its meaning, its causes, and the roost effective way to deal with it.

This exercise has been found most effective if practiced daily, preferably during the first hours of the day. Whenever possible, it is to be done shortly after waking up and considered as a symbolic *second awakening.* It is also of great value to repeat it in its brief form several times during the day, returning to the state of disidentified "I" consciousness.

The exercise may be modified appropriately, according to one's own purpose and existential needs, by adding stages of disidentification to include other functions besides the three fundamental ones (physical, emotional, mental), as well as subpersonalities, roles, etc. It can also begin with disidentification from material possessions. Some examples follow:

"I *have* desires, but I *am not* my desires. Desires are aroused by drives, physical and emotional, and by other influences. They are often changeable and contradictory, with alternations of attraction and repulsion; therefore they are not my *self.* I *have* desires, but I *am not* my desires." (This is best placed between the emotional and mental stage.)

"I engage in various activities and play many roles in life. I must play these roles and I willingly play them as well as possible, be it the role of son or father, wife or husband, teacher or student, artist or executive. But I am more than the son, the father, the artist. These are roles, specific but *partial* roles, which I, myself, am playing, agree to play, can watch and observe myself playing. Therefore I *am not* any of them. I *am self-identified,* and I am not only the actor, but the *director* of the acting."

This exercise can be and is being performed very effectively in groups.

The group leader voices the affirmations and the members listen with eyes closed, letting the significance of the words penetrate deeply.

BY KENNETH SØRENSEN

AWARENESS BASED MEDITATION

Disidentify from the body

Close your eyes and sit in a relaxed position. Let go of the body. Become the observer noting your body's various sensations: your skin's contact with your clothes, your bum on the chair, the air as you breathe, the sounds you hear, what you can smell and taste. Now observe your breath without trying to change it. Just observe without interfering.

As you sink completely into your body observe it and embrace it with affectionate appreciation...

That you can observe your body and its sensations shows that *you* are not your body but a consciousness using the body as a tool for experience and action.

Confirm to yourself: I have a body, I value it, but I am not my body.

Sit for a moment and let this realization sink in.

Now move your observation to the world of emotions

Disidentify from the emotions

Observe your emotions without judgement. Do not judge whether the emotions are good or bad, only observe them as temporary and changing. Are you excited, depressed, neutral, or something else?

Accept your emotions and create a loving space for them to simply be.

If *you* can observe your emotions, they cannot *be* you. *You* are a consciousness using your emotions as a tool for experience and action.

Confirm to yourself: *I have emotions, I value them, but I am not my emotions.*

Sit for a moment and let this realization sink in.

Now move your observation to the world of thought

Disidentify from the mind

Observe without judgement your mind, the thoughts, ideas, and images in your field of consciousness. You may think you have no thoughts, but *that* is a thought itself. See your thoughts as clouds drifting across an inner landscape.

Observe also the inner commentator, the voice inside you that you often associate with your own voice. Let it go.

Accept your thoughts and create a loving space where they can be, until they disappear ... and then release them.

That you can *observe* your thoughts shows that *you* are not your thoughts. Your thoughts are objects in consciousness. You are the thinker, not the thoughts.

Confirm to yourself: *I have a mind, I value my mind, but I am not my mind.*

Self-Identification

Who is observing your body, emotions and mind? It is the observer: you as pure self-awareness. *Who* is it that has intended and acted? You have, as will. You are, in other words, a center of pure self-awareness and will.

Say to yourself: *I am a center of pure self-awareness and will.*

Meditation as the observer

Now focus your awareness on the observer. This is obviously not possible, but the exercise itself will open you up to the source of awareness. Enter the eternal now, which is always pure awareness. Nothing is more important at this moment than to experience this awareness.

Let everything be as it is and then do a complete turn into the wakefulness of the moment.

Lovingly and *without judgement* let go of everything that enters your field of awareness, feelings, images, thoughts. No matter how beautiful or interesting it might be, let it go with determination and love.

If you lose focus or become identified with the content of consciousness let your breath be your anchor. Breathe through your body, emotions, and thoughts.

Focus your entire awareness on this quiet now, and move everything else to the background.

Anchoring

To close the meditation send awareness and positive energy out to your network.

BY KENNETH SØRENSEN

CREATIVE MEDITATION
on the Ideal Model: The Lotus of Peace and Harmony

Centering

Sit in a comfortable position and release the body. Become the observer noting your body's various sensations. Take the time to relax.

Observe your emotions and mood. Don't try to change anything, just observe. Step back; observe your thoughts and inner talk. Become aware of your thoughts and gradually let them go. The task is not to change your thought but to let them pass like clouds in the sky.

Observe your awareness and focus on its source. Recognise yourself as the observer.

Establish the self-Soul connection

Move your attention to the heart center. Visualise a brilliant blue-white light emanating a gentle, feminine energy throughout your entire being.

Once you feel the presence of this being, send the blue-white stream of heart energy to the center of your head, where there is also see a blue-white light. This now begins to enter and relax your brain cells.

From this point you connect with all the awakened souls in the world. Observe that you've become part of a network of forces helping and supporting each other.

When you have established this connection, draw the blue-white energy up to a wonderful sphere of light just above your head. This is your soul, your divine Self, which contains all that is good, true and beautiful.

Now, in your own way, invoke the divine. See how the pillar of blue-white light reaching from your heart to the point above your head gently fills your soul.

Identification with the Lotus of Peace and Harmony

Now turn your attention to the heart center, located between your shoulder blades and extending to the middle of the chest. Feel its softness and sink into its centre. Notice how this soft, feminine being slowly strengthens and fills your entire chest. Sense how it flows through your heart and connects you with all living beings.

See how this is an inner being of beauty and grace, how it radiates a love that opens all hearts through the gentle force of beauty.

Now visualise a beautiful white lotus bud in the middle of the blue-white light. Sense how it contains the essence of peace and harmony.

Feel it slowly open up, petal by petal, as a fragrance of peace and harmony spreads throughout your entire being.

Go deeper and deeper into your identification with this white lotus flower. Unite with its essence and become the spirit of peace and harmony yourself.

Anchoring

Send peace and harmony to your entire network and all living beings saying OM three times, loud and clear in three long breaths.

BY KENNETH SØRENSEN

THE SOUL-FLOW METHOD

The points outlined below need not be followed in the order given. This is a guideline and in practice the sessions can develop differently.

Choose a subpersonality to work with or start the exercise by focusing on a certain age or a role and allow one to appear.

Centring and the Healing Pillar

1. Become the observer, relax your body, be still and follow your breath.

2. Visualise a sun in your heart region, emanating acceptance and love throughout your personality.

3. Now visualise a golden light emanating from the sun in your heart, through your throat, and out through the top your head, where it reaches a golden sun above it. This is your soul and higher consciousness, containing all your wisdom. Ask your soul for guidance and wisdom.

4. Observe how the sun of the soul emanates a warm, loving light and wisdom throughout your body.

5. Notice how the energy flows through your body, legs, and feet, down to the core of the earth, Gaia. Here you contact the healing energies of Mother Earth. Gradually draw them back up to the heart through the same channel.

6. Center the energy from the soul and Mother Earth at the heart centre.

7. From your heart send a warm, loving energy to all your subpersonalities. Accept them and ask for their co-operation. Direct the energy towards your solar plexus.

Identification of the Subpersonality

Now focus on a problem, situation, feeling, or subpersonality and let it emerge into the light of the mind's eye.

Explore the subpersonality's situation, environment, strategy and needs. Approach it as a living being with whom you can have a dialogue.

Transformation of the Subpersonality

Hold the subpersonality in your heart and send it love and light.

Let it know that it is a valuable and loving part of you and your inner family of subpersonalities.

Let it know when it was created – at what age – and explain that it is stuck in a time warp and that you will now bring it to the present, making sure that it understands what you mean.

Explain that it has the same soul and purpose as you: to live a meaningful life in greater love and growth – chose your own formulations – and ask if it understands.

Let it know that it can be what it wants through the light it carries in its heart.

Explain how it can find its way to the heart through the light bridge connecting your two hearts. Visualise this light. Then ask if it can see it too. Explore the quality of the light.

Ask if it wants to enter your heart, so it can discover the transpersonal potential to become the best version of itself (perfect inner child, teenager etc.).

See the light flow from your soul to your heart, from your heart to the heart of the subpersonality, and back again to your soul – the sun above your head. Let the light flow in this triangle.

Integration of the Subpersonality

Visualise the subpersonality entering your heart. Surrender the process to the soul and watch the integration unfold.

Anchor it in the new reality by talking about its new life outside the time warp.

Anchor it in external reality – in the now – by giving it the role it has in your life. Explain how its qualities have a positive useful function in your life.

Synthesis

The synthesis is complete when the patterns restricting the client and his subpersonalities have become resolved into their opposites: when e.g. their loneliness has been transformed into a loving connection with the world.

BY KENNETH SØRENSEN

CREATIVE MEDITATION
on Intuitive Impressions

Preparation

Choose a topic for meditation into which you want deeper insight.

Centering

Sit in a comfortable position and let go of the body. Observe it various sensations. Take the time to relax completely.

Observe your emotions and mood. Change nothing, merely observe. Step back and observe your thoughts and inner talk. Note your thoughts and let them go, passing like clouds in the sky.

Observe your awareness and focus on its source. Recognise yourself as the observer.

Establish the self-Soul connection

Shift your attention to the heart center. Visualise a brilliant blue-white light emanating a gentle, feminine energy throughout your entire being.

Feel the presence of this being, and bring the blue-white energy stream from your heart up to the middle of the brain, where there is also a blue-white light. It now begins to relax your brain cells.

When you have established this connection, draw the blue-white energy up to a sphere of light just above your head. This is your soul, your divine Self, which contains all that is good, true and beautiful.

In this state of consciousness, find a quiet place of serenity and ask your soul to illuminate your topic of meditation. Let your awareness rest at the point above your head, in your head, or in the middle of the chest.

You are now totally open and alert. Your soul can now spark spontaneous flashes of understanding and insight into the subject matter. Be patient and confident. Do not think, but trust that your answer will come, perhaps now, or perhaps later, while walking or relaxing.

Anchoring

Send inner peace and harmony to your entire network and all living beings by saying OM three times, loud and clear in three long breaths.

REFERENCES

(You can find all articles marked with * at www.psykosyntese.dk)

- Assagioli, Roberto, 1934, *Loving Understanding*, The Beacon *

- Assagioli, Roberto, 1942, *Spiritual Joy*, The Beacon *

- Assagioli, Roberto, 1960, *The Education of Gifted and Super-Gifted Children*, Psychosynthesis Research Foundation. Issue No. 8 *

- Assagioli, Roberto, 1961, *Self Realization and Psychological Disturbances*, Psychosynthesis Research Foundation Issue No. 10 *

- Assagioli, Roberto, 1963, *Creative Expression in Education* (It's Purpose, Process, Techniques and Results) Psychosynthesis Research Foundation *

- Assagioli, Roberto, 1965, *Psychosynthesis: Individual and Social* (Some Suggested Lines of Research), Psychosynthesis Research Foundation, Issue No. 16 *

- Assagioli, Roberto, 1967a, *Psychosomatic Medicine and Bio-Psychosynthesis*, Psychosynthesis Research Foundation, Issue No. 21*

- Assagioli, Roberto, 1967b, *Jung and Psychosynthesis*, Psychosynthesis Research Foundation. Issue No. 19 *

- Assagioli, Roberto, 1968a, *Notes on Education*, Psychosynthesis Research Foundation *

- Assagioli, Roberto, 1968b, *The Science and Service of Blessing*, Sundial House *

- Assagioli, Roberto, 1969, *Symbols of Transpersonal Experiences*, Psychosynthesis Research Foundation, Reprint No. 11 *

- Assagioli, Roberto, 1970, *The Technique of Evocative Words*, Psychosynthesis Research Foundation, Issue No. 25 *

- Assagioli, Roberto, 1972, *The Balancing and Synthesis of Opposites*, Psychosynthesis Research Foundation, Issue No. 29) *

- Assagioli, Roberto, 1973, *The Conflict between the Generations and the Psychosynthesis of the Human Ages*, Psychosynthesis Research Foundation, Issue No. 31 *

- Assagioli, Roberto, 1974, *Training a Statement,* Florence: Istituto di Psicosintesi *

- Assagioli, Roberto, 1974, *The Act of Will,* Turnstone Press

- Assagioli, Roberto, 1975, *Psychosynthesis*, Turnstone Press

- Assagioli, Roberto,1975b, *The Resolution of Conflicts and Spiritual Conflicts and Crises*, Psychosynthesis Research Foundation, Issue No. 34 *

- Assagioli, Roberto, 1983a, *Psychosynthesis Typology*, Institute of Psychosynthesis *

- Assagioli, Roberto, 1983b, *Cheerfulness* (A Psychosynthetic Technique), Pasadena Calif.: Psychosynthesis Training Center *

- Assagioli, Roberto, 1983c, *Life as a Game and Stage Performance* (Role Playing) Pasadena Calif.: Psychosynthesis Training Center *

- Assagioli, Roberto, 2007, *Transpersonal Development*, Inner Way Productions

- Assagioli, Roberto, Undated 1, *Psychosynthesis in Education*, Psychosynthesis Research Foundation, Reprint No. 2 *

- Assagioli, Roberto, Undated 2, *Talks on the Self*, (Handed out from The Psychosynthesis and Education Trust, London) *

- Assagioli, Roberto, Undated 3, *The Superconscious and the Self*, The Psychosynthesis and Education Trust, London. Written by Jim Vargui, based on interview with RA *

- Assagioli, Roberto, Undated 4, *From the couple to the community*, (unknown source) *

- Assagioli, Roberto, Undated 5, *A Psychological Method for Learning Languages*, Psychosynthesis Research Foundation, Issue No. 3 *

- Assagioli, Roberto, Undated 6, *Discrimination in service*, (The Institute of Psychosynthesis, London) *

- Assagioli, Roberto, Undated 7, *Music as a Cause of Disease and as a Healing Agent*, Psychosynthesis Research Foundation, Issue No. 5 *

- Assagioli, Roberto, Undated 8, *Smiling Wisdom*, Psychosynthesis Research Foundation, Issue No. 4 *

- Assagioli, Roberto, Undated 9, *Synthesis in Psychotherapy*, Psychosynthesis Research Foundation, Issue No.15 *

- Assagioli, Roberto, Undated 10, *The Psychology of Woman and Her Psychosynthesis*, Psychosynthesis Research Foundation. Issue No. 24 *

- Assagioli, Roberto, Undated 11, *The Self a Unifying Center*, The Psychosynthesis and Education Trust, London *

- Assagioli, Roberto, Undated 12, *Training of the Will*, Psychosynthesis Research Foundation, Issue No. 17 *

- Assagioli, Roberto, Undated 13, *Transpersonal Inspiration & Psychological Mountain Climbing*, Psychosynthesis Research Foundation, Issue No. 36 *

- Assagioli, Roberto, Undated 14, *Transmutation and Sublimation of Sexual Energies*, Psychosynthesis Research Foundation, Issue No. 13 *

- Assagioli, Roberto, Undated 15, *What Is Synthesis?* (Handed out from The Psychosynthesis and Education Trust, London) *

- Assagioli, Roberto, Undated 16, *The Seven Ways* (Handed out from The Psychosynthesis and Education Trust, London) *

- Besmer, Beverly, *Height Psychology*: *Discovering the self and the Self*, Interpersonal Development, 4, 1973-4, pp. 215-225 *

- Brown, Molly Young, 2004, Unfolding Self, the Unfolding of Psychosynthesis, Helios Press

- Davidson, Gordon, 2011, Joyful Evolution, Golden Firebird Press

- Ferrucci, Piero, 1982, What We May Be, Tarcher/Putnam

- Ferrucci, Piero, 1990, Inevitable Grace, Tarcher/Putnam

- Ferrucci, Piero, 2014, Your Inner Will, Tarcher/Putnam

- Firman, John 1991, "I" And Self – Re-Visioning Psychosynthesis

- Firman, John & Gila, Ann, 1997, The Primal Wound, SUNY

- Firman, John & Gila, Ann, 2002, Psychosynthesis – A Psychology of the Spirit, SUNY

- Firman, John & Gila, Ann, 2004, A Suggested Change in the Egg Diagram

- Firman, John & Gila, Ann, 2007, Assagiolis Seven Core Concepts for Psychosynthesis Training

- Freund, Diana, 1983, Conversations with Roberto, Psychosynthesis Digest Spring issue *

- Hardy, Jean, 1996, A Psychology with a Soul, Woodgrange Press

- Miller, Stuart, 1972, The Will of Roberto Assagioli, Intellectual Digest, October *
1973, Miller, Stuart, The Rebirth of the Soul, Intellectual Digest, August, *

- Murphy, Michael, 2012, The Emergence of Evolutionary Panenteism: http://www.itp-international.org/library/print/emergence-evolutionary-panentheism

- Keen, Sam, 1974, The Golden Mean of Roberto Assagioli, Psychology Today Interview *

- Parfitt, Will, 2006, Psychosynthesis: The Elements and Beyond, PS Avalon

- Rowan, John, 1990, Subpersonalities – The People Inside Us, Routledge

- Rueffler, Margret, 1995, Our Inner Actors, PPPI Press

- Schuller, Michael, 1988, Psychosynthesis in North America

- Schaub, Bonney Gulino & Richard, 1994, Freedom in Jail, Assagiolis Notes. Bragt i onlinemagasinet Psychosynthesis Quarterly, Marts 2015.

- Schaub, Bonney Gulino & Richard, 2003, Dante's Path, Gotham Books

- Schaub, Bonney Gulino & Richard, 2013, Transpersonal Development, Florence Press

- Servan-Schreiber, Claude, 1974, A Higher View of The Man-Woman Problem, Synthesis 1*

- Sliker, Gretchen, 1992, Multiple Mind: Healing the Split in Psyche and World, Shamballa

- Smith Huston,1976, Forgotten Truth: The common Vision of the Worlds Religions, Harper San Francisco

- Sørensen, Kenneth, 2008, Integral Psychosynthesis a comparison of Wilber and Assagioli *

- Sørensen, Kenneth, 2016, Psychosynthesis and Evolutionary Panentheism *

- Tolle, Eckhart, 2004, The Power of Now, Namaste Publishing

- Vargui, James, 1974, Subpersonalities and psychotherapy *

- Visser, Frank, 1998 Transpersonal Psychology at a Crossroad, http://www.integralworld.net/esseng2.html (20.5.2008)

- Visser, Frank, 2003, Thought as Passion, SUNY

- Washburn, M. 1990, Two Patterns of Transcendence. Journal of Humanistic Psychology, 30 (3), pp.84-112.

- Wilber, Ken, 1999a, The Collected Works of Ken Wilber, Volume Two, Shambhala

- Wilber, Ken, 1999b, The Collected Works of Ken Wilber, Volume Three, Shambhala

- Wilber, Ken, 2000a, The Collected Works of Ken Wilber, Volume Seven, Shambhala

- Wilber, Ken, 2000b, The Collected Works of Ken Wilber, Volume Eight, Shambhala

- Wilber, Ken, 2000c, Integral Psychology, Shambhala

- Wilber, Ken, 2000d, A Theory of Everything, Shambhala

- Wilber, Ken, 2003, Excerpt G: Toward A Comprehensive Theory of Subtle Energies,

- Wilber, Ken, 2006, Integral Spirituality, Shambhala

- Whitmore, Diana, 2004, Psychosynthesis Counselling in Action, third edition, Sage

REFERENCES

CPSIA information can be obtained
at www.ICGtesting.com
Printed in the USA
BVHW060735040222
627989BV00004B/91